WORKING OUT YOUR OWN
BELIEFS

A Guide for Doing Your Own Theology

Douglas E. Wingeier

ABINGDON

Nashville

WORKING OUT YOUR OWN BELIEFS
A Guide for Doing Your Own Theology

Copyright © 1980 by Abingdon

Library of Congress Cataloging in Publication Data

Wingeier, Douglas E
　　Working Out Your Own Beliefs

　　Includes bibliographical references.
　　1. Theology, Doctrinal—Popular works.
I. Title.
BT77.W73　　　　　　230　　　　　　79-21097

ISBN 0-687-46190-1

Scripture quotations are from the Revised Standard
Version of the Bible, copyrighted 1946, 1952, © 1971,
1973 by the Division of Christian Education of the
National Council of the Churches of Christ in the U.S.A.
and are used by permission.

Versions of material in chapters 5 and 6 appeared earlier
in "Christian Education as Faith Translation," *The Living
Light*, Fall 1977.

MANUFACTURED BY THE PARTHENON PRESS AT
NASHVILLE, TENNESSEE, UNITED STATES OF AMERICA

TO CAROL

who taught me the necessity
of doing my own theology

Contents

Preface

Theology is the study of God. As such it is, or should be, of compelling interest to every Christian. But somehow through the centuries it became the particular province of professional clergy and theologians. Elaborate systems were devised, a knowledge of classical languages was required, and a specialized vocabulary was developed. All this demanded years of training and much time for study in order to turn theology into a resource for nurturing one's faith in God.

The scholars wrote books about dogmatic theology, systematic theology, philosophical theology, and biblical theology. The churches developed dogmas and creeds. And all the while, lay people just continued reading their Bibles, praying and worshiping God, affirming their beliefs, and trying to be faithful in applying them in everyday life.

Today, however, many lay persons no longer see the relevance of the Bible and Christian teaching to their daily lives. They live in a secular, fast-paced, materialistic world, in which the Bible appears as an outdated relic full of worthy ideas, but little practical guidance. When behavior is dictated by peer-group norms, and decisions must be made quickly, theology seems to be an idle pursuit.

At the same time, such persons feel uneasy about this lack of connection between life and religion. They are intelligent, thoughtful, and searching for a faith that will help them work through issues of value and priority they face everyday, and that they currently are resolving with largely secular, impromptu yardsticks. They are looking for some "handles," or guidelines, for thinking theologically about their lives. They want to find a way to rediscover the relevance of the Bible and the Christian faith to their everyday experience.

Disappointments, frustrations, choices, boring routines, conflict within relationships—these are daily occurrences. So are moments of joy, kindness, insight, and challenge. But for some, there is seldom an awareness that God is involved in all this, or that he cares. "Doing theology" can help reestablish this connection. To look at our daily experience from the perspective of Scripture and Christian understandings puts our life in a new light and shows us what God is doing in our midst.

Because most contemporary persons know their own experience best, the approach taken in this book is to start with that experience and to relate the resources of Scripture and tradition to it. This is not to imply that experience has priority as a test of truth. It is simply to follow the pattern in which our minds work. We experience things first, and then we try to understand them in the light of some system or framework of thought.

The intent of this book is to help us introduce biblical and theological perspectives into the framework we normally use to interpret, or make meaning of, our experience.

In recent years some theologians have discovered what lay people knew all along—that theology is not only a profound subject for study, but more importantly, it is an activity in which all Christians engage. The active terms "theologizing" and "doing theology" convey the idea that theology is not reserved to the scholar in the quiet solitude of his study, but rather is a process done in the push and pull of life.

"Doing theology" is reflecting on experience from the stance of faith, making use of the resources of Scripture and Christian tradition. It is a task, not just for specialists, but for the whole church.

No one can do your theology for you. Your experience is unique, and only your efforts to understand God's action in it will satisfy you fully. Of course, Bible helps and books on theology will give you some tools and insights for relating your faith to your life in a meaningful way. A list of these is provided in the back of this book. But unless you devote the time and energy needed to make theological meaning from your experience, your Sunday life and your weekday life will remain divorced, to some extent.

This book is intended to help you bridge that gap by providing a rationale and the tools for doing your own theology. Each chapter after the first, which introduces the problem and the approach, presents one aspect of a coordinated process of doing theology. Each contains some theoretical material, an illustration of how it might be applied by an ordinary American family, and practical exercises for theologizing both individually and in groups. Faith translation in decision-making, and the guidelines of experience, reason, Scripture, and tradition, are the five dimensions dealt with in this manner.

The theory and exercises in each chapter will stand on their own and can be used in a different order and without reference to the other chapters. We do not always experience life in a linear fashion, and the process of doing theology may be entered at any one of the four points. We can begin with Scripture, tradition, reason, or experience—as long as we touch base with the other three at some time during the process—and be assured that we will come out at pretty much the same place. But the chapters do have a cumulative sequence, so that the foundations laid in the early pages are helpful in making full and effective use of the later ones.

This book may be used either by individuals or by groups—as a study course, as a devotional guide, or for enrichment reading. The exercises at the end of each chapter are intended just to prime the pump. Similar ones may be found in the books mentioned in section D of the Resource List. Others may be invented readily by individuals or groups to meet their own needs and purposes. They may be followed either in full or in part as you first study the book, but they also can be repeated, adapted, or used with variations in your devotional life, journal-keeping, personal reflection, or ongoing group sharing.

This is not, in other words, the usual one-time study or reading book, but rather a resource to which you can return time and again for guidelines, suggestions, and a process for continuing to do your own theology.

It is written to and for lay people, and does not require a religious professional to lead you in study. If there are both ordained and lay persons in your group, you are encouraged to share as equals in the process of theologizing about your experience. Members with special backgrounds or training may offer their resources, but without speaking as authorities. Rotate the leadership among all members of the group, so that no one dominates and all may participate equally in the struggle to relate faith to life in meaningful ways.

Many persons have influenced me along the journey leading to this book. Special appreciation is expressed to: Dr. Ira Progoff of Dialogue House; Sister Ann Wylder of

Fullerton Cenacle House in Chicago; the Doctor of Ministry candidates at Garrett-Evangelical Theological Seminary who have shared their lives and meanings with me in deep and honest dialogue; Dr. Francis W. Boelter, Dr. Paul G. Rademacher, and Joanne Hoyt, who have read the manuscript and suggested helpful improvements; Martha Sherwood, my former secretary, who typed the manuscript; and countless lay persons in many local churches who have participated with me in doing theology and thereby have helped to shape the model presented here.

Doing my own theology has nurtured my growth as has nothing else in my life. It has helped me establish my identity, plant my roots, make clear choices, chart my vocational course, discover God's activity in my life, and become a more faithful witness. I hope it does half as much for you.

Douglas E. Wingeier

Chapter One

Can It Make Sense Again?

David was late for supper. Marge Adams, his mother, was annoyed, but had kept food hot for him. His father Walter and his younger sisters Sarah and Janet, had eaten and left for their evening activities.

It was nearly 8:30 when David sauntered in, explaining that he had stayed after school to complete an overdue assignment and then worked late at the supermarket to make up the lost time.

Marge knew he hadn't been doing well in school lately. Just that morning she had had a conference with his homeroom teacher. No motivation to study, behind in his work, poor class participation—it was the same story in every class.

David's attitude at home had changed, too; he seemed morose and uncommunicative. He took the phone into his room to talk, refused to go to church with the family, and barely nodded at his sisters when he passed them on the stairs.

David was in his last semester of high school, with life as a young adult just opening up, and yet he seemed so lifeless and depressed. Whatever could be wrong with him?

Marge poured herself a cup of coffee and sat down to talk with her son as he ate. She had to tell him the outcome of her conference at school and was determined to get to the bottom of his strange and uncharacteristic behavior.

At first David gave only grudging responses. Nothing was wrong. He was OK. It was his teachers who were at fault. The classes were boring. They treated him like a child. He was fed up with school.

But the more he talked, the more other things began to tumble out. He was uncertain about the future. He didn't feel ready for college, but he couldn't see another year as a full-time stock boy. He and Cindy had had a falling out over something—something he wanted, but she didn't. Then he let it slip that he had begun smoking pot pretty regularly.

Marge was shocked and didn't know how to respond. She had never talked with her son at this level before and couldn't handle the situation. She would wait until Walter got home and discuss it with him. But no, on second thought—he would only fly into a rage and storm into David's room. David would just retreat back into his shell, and who knows when she might reach him again.

She was stymied. Where could she turn? Her heart was heavy. How could she help her son?

A familiar scene? Yes indeed. The details may be different, but such problems are faced by countless present-day families. We attend church regularly. Our children are brought up in Sunday school. We have heard a thousand sermons. We even may attend an adult Bible class. But when things go wrong, when situations arise that we don't know how to handle, our faith does not seem to help us.

Marge does not realize that her present family situation

12

can be understood in terms of the biblical theme of alienation and reconciliation. She does not see the correlation between David's experience and that of the prodigal son in need of a forgiving father. She does not grasp that Walter's anger toward David, and his workaholism, which had taken him back to the office tonight, are rooted in his low self-esteem, similar to that which led the little tax collector Zacchaeus to exploit his neighbors and thus feel a need for the forgiveness of Jesus. Nor does she understand that her own perplexity is like that of Martha, who was "anxious and troubled about many things," but had neglected the "one thing . . . needful" (Luke 10:41,42).

When we as church people are unable to correlate our faith with our everyday experience, we tend to "lose faith in faith." It doesn't help us when we need it. So we may drop out of the church and stop pretending. Or we may continue to go through the motions—worship, church school, committee work, choir—feeling increasingly guilty. Our prayers seem empty. The creeds we recite speak of realities we no longer feel. We sing the hymns, but there is no answering song of joy in our hearts.

We feel like hypocrites, yet we are good people. We haven't done anything ugly or sinful. We just wonder why a religion that promises so much, and that formerly meant a great deal to us, now seems to deliver so little. Can it ever make sense again?

If we are to find new meaning in our Christian faith and have it serve once more as a helpful resource for our everyday living, we first need to understand our situation. Why is this loss of meaning a common experience for people today?

Society Encourages It

We live in a society that encourages alienation. Our environment is constructed with replaceable parts. Appliances, jobs, homes, people—we just plug in a substitute and things are supposed to work as well as new. We are separated from one another and from our world. We live in locked apartment buildings and communicate through intercoms. Our parental homes are miles away. Between rubber tires and concrete pavements, our feet never touch the earth. We fire some workers and hire others. Our children groove on rock music, while we attend the symphony. We experience life through the TV tube. We cannot explain to our families what we do all day. We fail to connect the various segments of our existence, and then wonder why we have trouble relating faith to life.

The root sickness beneath all this is self-serving individualism. Our first loyalty is to ourselves. We must "do our own thing," find personal fulfillment, seek ways to meet our own needs, serve our own interests. We have distorted the "uniqueness of the individual" doctrine so that rights take precedence over responsibilities, and enjoyment over commitments. Our worth has priority over our relationships.

We are a society of isolated individuals, going our own way. We will believe what we choose and do as we please. We do not discuss our values and faith with one another. That would be an invasion of privacy. So when the chips are down, we are unable to verbalize our faith, even to clarify our own situation. Nor can we share it with a friend in time of need.

This creates a vast quagmire of pluralistic in beliefs. There is no sense of community built around a common faith. We are confused about what to believe. The old faith that once formed an organizing principle for our life is under attack from every direction. There are so many competing value systems and life-styles that we no longer know what is right. We are confronted with Transcendental Meditation to replace *The Upper Room*, encounter groups instead of prayer meetings, liberation movements in place of salvation, and

14

Hare Krishnas on the street corners, reversing the Christian mission to other countries.

It is important that persons be free to affirm their own beliefs. But this multiplicity of faiths and behavior patterns is bewildering to any who lack the tools to translate old values into new situations. Having lost the security of a system of widely held beliefs, we do not know how to do our own theology. We do not have the skills to make meaning out of our own life experience in such a way as to guide our decisions and sustain us in times of crisis.

Furthermore, our busy, hectic life leaves little time for reflection. We move rapidly from one event to another, without asking what it all means. We do not realize that it is not making sense, because we are too busy piling one experience on top of another, like bricks on a wall. But because we have not fastened the bricks together with the mortar of meaning, the wall comes toppling down at the first sign that things are not working out as planned.

There is so much stimulation around us that it is easier just not to think about the meaning of things. We can listen to the radio while we drive, watch TV while we are cooking, go to a movie instead of staying home with a book, and then flop into bed rather than kneeling to pray. The ads tell us what to buy; the travelogs, where to go; the commentators, what is happening; the community calendar, how to spend our time; and the radio preachers, what to believe. We do not reflect on the fact that, every day, we move a step closer to death. Things are not making sense, but we don't worry about it. We don't ask the all-important question, Why?

The Church Supports It

Such a situation is made to order for a certain type of church and church leader. When we are bewildered, the church can point the way. When we hunger for certainty and direction, the church can say, "The Bible says . . ." When we feel dependent and think we need an authority to say "Come unto me," the church can provide that authority and cultivate our dependence by telling us what to believe.

Such a church does not acknowledge that this is not all we need in order to become mature, decisive, responsible Christians. It tells us that to be good Christians, we must believe what it teaches. It attempts to provide direction without the freedom to choose, thereby undermining our capacity to discover for ourselves the resources in our faith and to make sense out of our own experience. Of course, not all churches operate this way. But those that do, reinforce our inability to work out our own beliefs.

Religious professionals sometimes contribute further to our sense of inadequacy, out of their own need to care for people. They are trained to provide us with pastoral care, interpret the Scriptures, and pass on the traditions. Their sermons do our religious thinking for us. They run effective programs, in which we participate as directed. They make regular pastoral calls, during which they pray for us and advise us on solutions to our problems. Wittingly or unwittingly, they encourage us to depend on them to act on our behalf in areas of faith and morals. If we let it happen, we may find ourselves relying more and more on our pastors and priests to interpret the meaning of the Bible and doctrine for us.

At still another point the church supports our inability to think theologically about our own lives. Through the centuries it has contributed to a deep division between faith and life. The medieval church exercised authority over all life. But it could not maintain that degree of power long. In an effort to carve out an area where it could reign supreme, it divided life into two realms—the sacred and the secular. The former became the province of the church, and at times it has shown little concern for the latter. Individuals could live as they pleased in the secular arena, as long as they said confession and did penance at church. "The world is not my home; I'm just a-passin' through." The church's task was, and still is, to save souls for heaven, not to become involved in "dirty politics" here on earth.

This has not been the stance of all branches of the church; many have taken God's mission to the world seriously. But it has been the dominant trend.

The result is that we do not think naturally of the relationship between faith and everyday life. Religion belongs in church on Sundays; then we get on with the tough business of making a living during the rest of the week. The Bible is a book written long ago about people who didn't have to face our kind of complex world. It is nice to have our children sing "Jesus Loves Me" and to hear the twenty-third Psalm. But it is just not practical to think that our Christian faith has much to do with shopping in the supermarket, running a punch press, or doing our algebra homework.

This attitude is understandable, given the separation between faith and life based on a dualism of soul and body taught by the church itself. But it doesn't help us much in our quest for meaning. It still leaves us asking, Can it make sense again?

We Ourselves Permit It

It is too easy to lay all the blame for our ineptness in doing theology at the door of others. To be sure, the pluralism and individualism of our culture are bewildering, and the attitudes of dependency and dualism cultivated by the church are seductive. But in the final analysis, it is we who either resist or submit to these tendencies.

Actually, religion as we are accustomed to it meets many of our needs very well. In a world where I am often only a statistic, and where even my next-door neighbor doesn't know my name, it is reassuring to find people in church who really care about me and to hear from the pulpit that "I am somebody." Coming from a household where my daughter is doing yoga or from an airport encounter with some Moonies, it is good to be able to stand and recite, "I believe in God the Father Almighty . . ." Having left the breakfast dishes in the sink, glanced at a headline about crime in the streets, and argued with Susie about what dress she should wear, it is consoling to sink into the pew and hear the familiar strains of "How Great Thou Art." And having had to struggle with the checkbook, resist pressure from the boss to falsify an order, or cope with sexual feelings toward someone else's spouse, it is comforting to hear the preacher's resounding, "Thus saith the Lord."

We sense that to try to relate our faith to our daily life would require real effort and courage. We would have to take time to pray, reflect on our experience, and become more familiar with the Bible and Christian beliefs. And we would need to make our through-the-week behavior more consistent with our Sunday affirmations. There could be some risk in this. So, for good reasons, we allow the weeks and years to go by, with the gap between our beliefs and our everyday experience remaining, or growing wider.

But we are uneasy about this. We know that our children in school are learning to "think mathematically." On the job, we are encouraged to "think profits." We could not make it as an engineer, a nurse, or a newspaper reporter, if we did not integrate the principles of sound physics, anatomy, or grammar into the practice of our profession. We know that if we are serious about being full-time Christians, we must make a habit of thinking theologically about our life. If we really want it to "make sense again," we must begin "doing theology" in earnest.

But it is not just an uneasy feeling or a comparison with

18

other disciplines that urges on us the necessity of correlating faith with life. For it is God himself who calls us to love him "with all your mind" (Mark 12:30). To be a faithful Christian requires us to put on biblical "spectacles" in order to experience life through the eyes of faith. As Paul puts it, we are to have "the eyes of your hearts enlightened, that you may know what is the hope to which he has called you" (Eph. 1:18). We are invited to "have this mind among yourselves, which is yours in Christ Jesus" (Phil. 2:5). We are to establish our identity as followers of Christ, and then to live out that self-understanding in all our relationships.

It is only as we actively cultivate our faith that we increasingly will come to understand events from a Christian perspective. Only then will things begin to make sense again.

Chapter Two

Translating Faith into Our Decisions

David Adams is deciding what to do after high school. His father is deciding whether to remain in a job that is no longer challenging. His mother Marge is deciding how to model the meaning of womanhood for her daughters. As a family, the Adams are deciding how to be supportive and accepting as they go through a time of crisis.

A key area where our faith intersects with our everyday experience is in decision-making. We follow some kind of guidelines in making our decisions. The criterion may be what's in it for us, what's good for business, or what will protect our reputation. We may choose on the basis of what our conscience tells us is right, what the neighbors will think, or what others are doing. As Christians, we will also look for resources to guide our choices in the teachings of the Bible and the church.

Because many of the life situations and moral dilemmas we face are unique to our time, however, we will not be able to carry over intact the doctrinal statements and ethical injunctions from an earlier era. We cannot make decisions in twentieth-century America on the basis of theological thinking done in sixteenth-century Germany or eighteenth-century England. Instead, we will need to translate the meaning made out of experience in those times into words and thought-forms that make sense to us today.

This is "faith translation," which may be defined as *the process of making meaning out of our experience, in the light of the root sources of faith in Scripture and tradition.*

We continually engage in meaning-making. Growing up in a certain culture, we discover categories of thought which help us to understand and interpret our experience. We learn colors, tastes, relationships, and values, and that knowledge aids us in determining whether a thing is red or blue, sweet or sour, heavy or light, right or wrong.

If we grow up in a Christian environment, we also gather reference points for meaning-making from the Bible, from church school lessons and worship services, and from relationships with other Christians. By means of these we are able to make theological meaning out of our experience. We know what is meant by "a Damascus-Road experience," "crossing the Jordan," and "by the waters of Babylon." The cross, the alpha and omega sign, the fish, and the chalice become symbols of great and lasting significance. Jonah, Mary Magdalene, and Nicodemus are familiar characters to us, and we begin to see qualities in ourselves that are similar to theirs. We discover that phrases such as "justification by faith," "the priesthood of all believers," and "the covenant community" grew out of concrete situations in church history and conveyed a wealth of meaning to Christians in those times, and even today.

When we become embroiled in the tense, fast-paced, secular life of our contemporary world, however, we are tempted to cast aside these images and categories as irrelevant. How could people who lived in tents, traveled on foot, or spoke in "thees" and "thous" have anything useful to say to us in this day of transistors and moon shots?

We have neglected one all-important step—faith translation. We have learned the biblical story and theological categories. And we take our present-day experience seriously enough. But we have lost the link that ties them together. That link is faith translation. We need to learn how to uncover the kernel of meaning that Christians in other ages found in their experience, peel away the outer crust of language and expression in which it was communicated, and find fresh, relevant ways of expressing it to people today.

Or, to move in the opposite direction, we can reflect on our present experiences, discover what these say about who we are and what life is all about, and then look for biblical images and theological themes that will ground these in our faith tradition. Both approaches are ways of doing theology.

Let us take a closer look at faith translation and discover how it helps in our decision-making. The process involves certain assumptions and procedures.

Faith translation assumes	*Faith translation involves*
1. the *unity* of faith and life.	1. discovering *crossing points* between revelation and event.
2. learning through *enculturation*.	2. developing an awareness of how ideas are *culturally conditioned*.
3. *theological pluralism*.	3. communication in a *cross-cultural* situation.
4. *everyone* is a theologian.	4. employing an *inductive* approach to theology.
5. *questions* are more "growthful" than answers.	5. asking, What's *meaningful* to me?

22

6. faith is biblical and theological *content*, plus experience.

6. utilizing *Scripture, tradition, reason,* and *experience* as guidelines for doing theology.

7. a *community* setting.

7. sharing and testing meanings in *dialogue* with other Christians.

1. Crossing Points Between Faith and Life

Faith translation assumes the unity of faith and life and engages us in looking for points of intersection between God's creative, redemptive purpose and the events around us. The dualistic split between sacred and secular has no place here. We expect God's presence and activity, not only in church and in heaven, but in everyday happenings here on earth.

Hence, God is active in our decision-making. Just as he led the people of Israel out of slavery in Egypt, so he is active in liberation movements today. The Spirit of new birth whom Jesus pointed Nicodemus toward is the same Spirit who transforms our life through a love relationship or a mid-life crisis. Even as Jesus invited the rich young ruler to "sell all that you have and distribute to the poor . . . and come, follow me" (Luke 18:22) and grieved when the young man went away sorrowful, so he is calling us to share with those in need and is saddened when we turn from him to take care of our own first.

God is ever present with us, affecting the course of events through the decisions of his people. It is up to us to discern the crossing points between his activity in the past and what is going on now, and then to describe them in ways that make sense to people today. This is faith translation.

23

2. Learning Through Cultural Conditioning

We like to think that we are consciously aware of all we learn, that we deliberately choose what to believe, and that we freely decide our behavior and life-style. Our freedom of thought and action is more limited than we suppose, however, for our minds are filled with messages that interpret the raw data of experience for us. Because the Amharic language has only three words for color, the Ethiopian people see only three colors. Because tribal peoples believe that a vital force inhabits all objects, for them the world is alive, and they will not cut down a tree or tear up the earth. Because our children watch football on TV and compete for grades in school, they experience life in terms of "the survival of the fittest" and "to the victor belong the spoils." When we hear and assimilate words like "trust," "achievement," and "creativity," these become important values for us.

Our minds are not blank tablets on which God writes messages intended just for us. We are scripted with a set of habits, thought-forms, and life goals before we even start to do our own theology. Our cultural conditioning affects the way we see objects and events. Our perceptions, ideas, and decisions are shaped by what our society has taught us.

This is true also of every biblical writer, theologian, and preacher who ever lived. So for the writer of Exodus, the crossing of the Red Sea by means of signs and wonders was a natural event, because in his culture it was normal to expect God to act that way. The psalmist and the writers of Judges and Kings believed that God commanded the slaughter of their enemies, because in their world every god championed the cause of his tribe, regardless of the cost. For a world-view in which emotional disturbance was understood as demon possession, the restoring of people to sanity through the casting out of demons was a common occurrence. A nomadic people who tended flocks and moved through the desert from oasis to oasis naturally would refer to their relationship with God in terms like "good shepherd," "green pastures," and "living water." Persons with a legal background would tend to use words such as "justification" and "atonement" to explain God's dealings with humanity.

And in our own day, when women are becoming increasingly conscious of past discriminations and their unique identity, it is natural for them to object to being included with "mankind" and to singing "Faith of Our Fathers." Blacks, Third World peoples, and other minorities, struggling against prejudice and economic exploitation, respond to the image of Jesus as a liberator. Schooled in the rational, linear mind-set, we define life and faith in terms of logical propositions, neglecting the element of feeling in biblical imagery and in the stained-glass window. Because of the commercial and technological orientation of our society, when facing a church or a personal decision, we ask What will it cost? or How can it be done? before even thinking about Why? and Who will it affect?

So we always need to be aware that our interpretations and decisions are strongly influenced by our cultural "spectacles." God's revelation is received, recorded, and communicated by human agents whose perceptions of his message are colored by the thought-forms and social patterns of their culture. This realization should make us exceedingly humble about claiming too much certainty as to "truth" or "what the Lord wants me to do."

3. Communication in a Pluralistic Setting

Since experience and cultural conditioning are different for each person, whenever we talk about our beliefs and values, we are in a cross-cultural situation. The same words have different meanings, and the same experience is given various interpretations.

For a Wisconsin farm boy, a square meal consists of meat, potatoes, and vegetables. He can't understand why his Georgia-born wife keeps serving him beans, cabbage, and corn bread for dinner. One person doesn't give a thought to shouting up the stairway; for another, it is the height of impropriety. To the older generation, it was important to remain a virgin until marriage; to the young, premarital sex within a caring relationship does not seem to raise a moral issue.

For some, Christian worship is not complete without the Eucharist; others stay away from church on Communion Sunday. Some think of the Bible as the "Word of God"; others equate this phrase with Jesus Christ, the Word made flesh.

Hence, in faith translation we must first understand how our unique cultural conditioning has affected our patterns of thought and expression. Then we will try to sort out the meaning we and others intend to transmit, from the forms of expression in which it is clothed.

Communication or decision-making in any group setting—family, church, or community—requires a sensitivity to these cultural "spectacles." Only thus can genuine understanding or consensus be achieved.

4. Everyone Does Theology Inductively

For centuries we were awed by the scholarly theologian who used big words, wrote big books, and had a big reputation. He was somehow in a class by himself, and we were duly impressed by our pastors who quoted from his books and explained to us in the pew what he meant. Today, however, for several reasons, there are no "big name" theologians around.

First, we now realize that their thought was conditioned by their historical situation, filtered through their individual experience, and therefore might not speak meaningfully to persons in other times and places.

Second, our cultural consensus has now collapsed, and no one system of theology is adequate to communicate about God's activity with all his people. We need the existentialists, the liberationists, the evolutionists, the classicists, and the process theologians, as well as the Wesleyans, the Calvinists, the Thomists, and all the other "-ists," because there are always some of us to whom a particular brand of theology makes sense.

Third, life is so complex and there are so many data in our human experience that no single theological system can possibly explain them all adequately. The "God of the gaps" approach, wherein concepts of God were used to explain all the conundrums of human experience, is no longer viable. For a theologian to attempt to develop a system of thought to explain everything is an impossible dream.

Finally, we have realized that many of the great thinkers, for all their scholarship, did their theology much the same way we do. They started with their everyday experience and tried to make sense of it in relation to the Bible and Christian teaching. Whether the event was an apple falling on the head, a life-changing conversion, the premature loss of a loved one, or an illness that dragged on year after year, it was the experience that started them thinking and eventually resulted in a theological statement. Or they tested the teachings of Scripture and doctrine against their experience. Their books might suggest that they thought it all up out of their heads with ease, but the glimpses we get into their lives reveal a faith and theology that emerged through sweat and struggle.

They did theology inductively. And so do we. We all start with the data of experience and *induce* meaning from it. We

27

put together several experiences, discover their common thread, give the result a name, and speak of it as though the name were the reality.

John Wesley went into a little chapel on Aldersgate Street, found peace from the turmoil in his life, spoke of having his "heart strangely warmed," and ever since, we have described a whole range of conversion experiences in terms of the "warm heart."

Some persons, exposed to the baptism of the Holy Spirit, speak in "unknown tongues." Just as Columbus, sailing for India, met some strange people on a distant shore and assumed they were Indians, so some might jump to the conclusion that only those who speak in tongues can know the Spirit.

The point right now is not whether our meanings and decisions are correct. It is that we are less likely to deduce them from some eternal, God-given truth than we are to discover them inductively through reflecting on our experience.

5. Asking Questions

We grow by asking questions, not by getting answers. We help others grow by asking questions, not by giving answers. We do theology by asking, What's meaningful to me in this experience?—not by looking up a theological explanation in some book of doctrine. We make decisions, not by asking a pastor or other authority figure to tell us what to do, but by using biblical and theological guidelines to help us know the right questions to ask ourselves about a situation. And then we test our conclusions against the thought and experience of others in the Christian community.

It is the process of searching that generates growth. Arrival at a destination affords only temporary satisfaction, for we discover that an interpretation that met our needs at one stage of our development soon loses its validity for us. We are like animals that shed their skins as they outgrow them.

For example, a young man believes that "separation from the world"—refusing to smoke, drink, dance, or go to movies—is a valid and necessary Christian life-style for him. Later on, however, he is led to consider "involvement in the world"—social action and full acquaintance with the best and worst of his culture—as imperative. Still later, he discovers that a balanced rhythm between involved service and reflective withdrawal is best. He is always asking, How can I be a faithful Christian? But the answer changes as he grows, and no one life-style is lastingly right for him.

So faith translation is tentative and searching. No decision about either belief or behavior is final. The meanings that emerge are fragile and indefinite. They provide guidance for awhile, but we are reluctant to impose them on others. The quest for fuller meaning goes on and can be either frustrating or invigorating, depending on the attitude we bring to it.

6. Content in Dialogue with Experience

When we speak of the Christian faith, we often mean a body of doctrine. To be a Christian means to believe certain things. But faith is much more than belief; it is the experience of trust and commitment, as well. "Belief" is the word we use to describe the meaning this experience has for us.

Jesus did not say, "By this all people will know that you are my disciples, that you recite the Apostles Creed," or "believe my teachings," or "accept the doctrine that I am born of a virgin." His test of discipleship was "if you have love for one another" (John 13:35). For him, loving relationships were

29

more important than correct beliefs, though his belief about God did help define the nature of true love.

Faith translation involves both relationships and beliefs. It calls for dialogue between experience and interpretation. We see a gorgeous sunset and have an inspiring feeling, and we call it a religious experience. We have a nasty argument and feel out of sorts and lonely, and we discover that sin is separation. We try reading the Bible from Genesis to Revelation and find that it uses archaic language, and we conclude that it is out-of-date. We see a film on migrants and hear a sermon on God's justice, and we decide to boycott a company that mistreats its workers.

Again, the issue is not the rightness or wrongness of our decisions and conclusions, but whether we have tested our experience against the content of Scripture and Christian teaching, and whether these help make sense of our life.

Some Christian theologians have built these elements into a formula for doing theology. They have suggested four sources, or guidelines, for theological reflection: Scripture, tradition, reason, and experience—with Scripture having priority. Any decision or belief, to be both sound and relevant, must be based on the Bible, consistent with church teachings, stated in a rational way, and compatible with our experience. All Christians are called to do their own theology, utilizing these guidelines. Differences of religious interpretation and practice are accepted, as long as these four criteria are observed.

Let us illustrate the use of these guidelines in everyday decision-making. Suppose you are thinking of buying a second car. Your recent experience suggests both the need for the car and a shortage of funds. The story of the rich young ruler and Jesus' statement that a person's "life does not consist in the abundance of . . . possessions" (Luke 12:15b) might commend frugality, and passages like those in II Corinthians 8 and 9 urge sharing your abundance with those in need. You find examples in the Christian tradition of both those who took the vow of poverty and those who lived in splendor. However, it seems reasonable, given your family's transportation needs, that you acquire a second car. Obviously, the evidence and the direction from these four sources are not in agreement. So you need to weigh their relative merits, consult with friends you trust, talk it through in a church sharing group, pray about it, and then risk your family decision in the direction supported by most of the guidelines. Finally, you must be ready to seek and accept God's forgiveness if it turns out that you have decided wrongly. A diagram may help to make this formula clear.

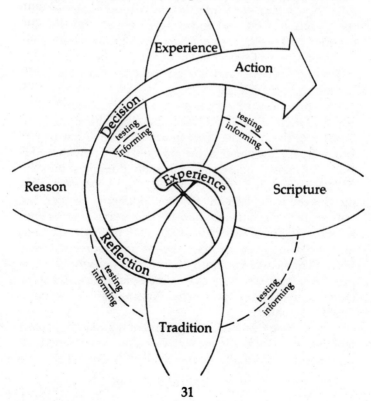

We make a decision to act on the basis of reflection on an experience. In our reflection we make use of our rational faculties and consult reference points in the Bible, the heritage of Christian doctrine, and our own previous experience. The guidance we receive from each of these sources is both informed by, and tested against, the other three. And our interpretation of the experience, our decision, and our action are informed and tested by all four.

7. Testing in the Community

The setting for doing theology is the covenant community. Our decisions and interpretations must be shared with the people of God and tested against their thought and experience. Theology is not a private affair. Rather, it is the mutual process of reflection on experience by which we in the church discover and test our understanding of God's nature and purpose.

"No prophecy of scripture is a matter of one's own interpretation" (II Peter 1:20). In fact, the Bible itself is the product of the historical community of faith. As we share and compare our personal insights and choices with others in the Christian community, our individual meanings are mutually enriched and corrected. An experience that puzzles me may be clearly understood by my brother. My sister may have an insight into a Scripture passage that has left me cold. Those who have studied our history and creeds may be able to help the rest of us appreciate why Presbyterians take communion in the pews, why Baptists practice immersion, why only some Episcopalians observe closed communion, and why Nazarenes are called a "holiness" church.

The covenant is a bond or agreement that ties Christians together and that binds us all to God. We are "the body of Christ and individually members of it" (I Cor. 12:27). We have a variety of gifts and contribute them willingly "to equip the saints for the work of ministry, for building up the body of Christ" (Eph. 4:12). We take responsibility for one another by testing our beliefs and choices against our pooled wisdom and experience with God and with the world.

The church strives, not for uniformity or agreement in interpretation, but for a unity of spirit and purpose, which enables us to accept differences and work together in God's mission. Jesus did not say, "A new commandment I give to you, that you believe the Bible and accept my teachings," but rather "that you love one another" (John 13:34). This understanding of the church emphasizes the *conciliar*, as contrasted with the *confessional* principle. A confessional church has a statement of faith to which all members must give assent. Persons in a conciliar church, on the other hand, practice responsible doctrinal pluralism. They stress a living relationship with Christ and faithful discipleship as the only sound bases for Christian fellowship.

This approach avoids dogmatism, on the one hand, and indifference, on the other. It does not create a permissive climate with no guidelines, in which people think as they please. Rather, it respects theological diversity and the freedom of members to do their own faith translation, remaining responsible to Scripture, tradition, reason, and experience.

The outcome of this corporate effort at doing theology is not conformity, or even full agreement, but rather a sense of commonality and shared meaning. To share meanings is to seek to understand the significance an experience has for someone else, even though it may mean something quite different to me. It is to listen and learn from one another, to support our individual quests for meaning, and to celebrate the discoveries we make along the way. It is to affirm one another as fellow seekers after God, "for in him we live and move and have our being" (Acts 17:28).

33

We now turn to some ways for you to practice faith translation, both by yourself and in a group.

TO DO IN PRIVATE

Begin a journal so that you can write down your reflections and keep them for future reference. Keep a looseleaf or spiral notebook for this purpose near your Bible and this book.

This exercise may be titled "My Decision." Think of an important decision you now face or have made recently. It could be a major purchase, a job possibility, a new relationship or life-style, a plan to leave home, post-retirement projects, a committee assignment, or some other matter. Write a brief paragraph describing the background leading up to the decision, your alternative choices, and the factors supporting and opposing each of them.

Next, write brief responses to the following:

1. How did(do) you feel during and/or after the decision-making process?

2. What values did(will) you say yes to by this decision?

3. What values did(will) you say no to?

4. What was(is) God trying to say to you through this process?

5. In what ways is your decision consistent or inconsistent with (a) the message of the Bible? (b) the teachings of the church? (c) your own best thinking? (d) your experience of God's guidance?

Now, what new insights have you gained through this exercise in faith translation? Are there any changes you want to make? Any new steps you need to take?

Spend some time in prayer, thanking God for any new

wisdom he has given you, asking his guidance for any unresolved issues, and seeking his strength for any difficult tasks that now must be undertaken.

TO DO IN A GROUP

An existing group, such as a church school class, men's fellowship, women's circle, or youth prayer group, can learn to do theology together in a better way. Or a new group may be organized just for this purpose. Learning to do theology can be the enrichment dimension of your group's next weekend retreat or summer camping experience. Or it can form the basis for your family devotions. But do develop some group with whom to share your individual theologizing and test your interpretations and decisions.

If the members of your group have not done the individual translation of faith into decision, then try this exercise so that everyone will have had a recent experience in choosing.

Arrange circles of chairs in three corners of the room, with the group sitting in the middle. As each statement is read, members decide which of the three conclusions best satisfies them, and go to the circle designated for those agreeing with that conclusion. Persons who can accept none of the three may remain in the center area. When all have made their choices, persons in each circle discuss why they chose as they did. Then go back to the middle of the room, read out the next statement, and repeat the process.

Here is a starter list of statements. Feel free to add, revise, or substitute to suit the needs and interests of your group.

1. God to me is (a) the Creator of the universe, who has made a beautiful world for me to enjoy and take care of; (b) a loving Parent who nurtures and forgives me; (c) a righteous Judge who rewards and punishes in terms of his perfect standards of right and wrong. (Those who agree with (a) go

to the first circle, those who prefer (b) go to the second, and those who affirm (c) to the third. Those who can accept none of the three form a circle where they are.)

2. To me the Bible is (a) the word of God that contains his plan of salvation; (b) a record of the history of Israel and the early church, describing their growing relationship with God; (c) a collection of stories of people like me, who sin and find reconciliation with a loving Father.

3. My attitude toward the church is that it is (a) a human organization dedicated to serving God; (b) a group established for worship, fellowship, and service; (c) the body of Christ, a community of people called by God to be a redemptive fellowship.

4. My view of world religions is that (a) they are all human efforts to search for God; (b) each contains some truth about God and what it means to be fully human, but none has the whole truth; (c) all are of equal validity in leading us to God—it is only an accident of birth that I am a Christian.

5. In my mind Jesus is (a) a good man, a prophet of God, a wise teacher; (b) the Messiah, Son of God, and Savior of the world; (c) my personal Savior and Lord.

6. For me, being a Christian means I should (a) repent, believe in the Lord Jesus Christ, and be baptized; (b) lead a good life, observe the Ten Commandments, and do unto others as I would have them do unto me; (c) be responsible in my commitments, love and be loved by God and by others, and give myself in service to those in need.

After making and discussing several of these choices, reflect individually on the experience. In a prayerful mood, complete the following sentences:

1. *Lord, I feel* —— (Describe how you feel about this experience in decision-making.)

2. *Lord, I am* —— (Describe the kind of person you are as indicated by the choices you have made.)

3. *Lord, I want to be* ——— (Describe the areas in which you want to grow as a result of what you have just learned about yourself and your beliefs.)

4. *Lord, help me to* ——— (Describe the steps you intend to take to develop your life and faith.)

Now take turns telling the group about your private reflections. If your responses are too personal to share, you may always "pass."

While one person is sharing, other members can help by (1) listening carefully and with understanding; (2) responding supportively and without criticism; (3) mentioning Scripture passages or theological ideas that help interpret the speaker's experience; (4) sharing comparable experiences as a way of expressing solidarity with the speaker; and (5) asking questions that help the speaker clarify thinking, identify alternatives, and determine next steps.

Be sure to allocate the time so each member who wishes is able to share reflections and receive a caring response from the group. Close with sentence prayers, expressing insights gained, support received, needs discovered, and decisions made.

OTHER EXERCISES

As alternatives, or to guide future personal reflection or group sharing, try these.

1. "Values and behavior." List the ten values you affirm most strongly. Check the two you have used most frequently in the past week to guide your decisions and behavior. Which two seem hardest to actualize? Where in the Bible is each of these values affirmed? Share these reflections with another person, and then with the group. What word from the Lord comes to you out of this experience?

2. "My life goals." Each person will need five 3 X 5 cards.

In the center of each card write a goal that you hope to accomplish in your lifetime (or in a stated period of time, such as three or five years). Arrange the cards in order of their importance to you, and write the rank of each, 1 through 5, in the upper left-hand corner. Next, in the lower left-hand corner of each card, write an A if this is a goal you must accomplish alone, or a C if it is something you must do cooperatively with others. Then, in the lower right-hand corner of each card, write the date when you hope you will have achieved the goal. Finally, in the upper right-hand corner, write a word or phrase that expresses the kind of help (from God or from others) that you will need in order to reach this goal.

If you are doing this in a group, select two cards you would like to share with others. Hold one in each hand so they can be seen, and look at one another's cards. Pair up with another person whose goals are similar to yours and share in more depth the thoughts behind what you have written on your cards. Then, reassemble as a total group and debrief the experience, voicing feelings, learnings, and common goals and needs.

Finally, as individuals, complete the following sentences:
I am the kind of person who ———
God is calling me to ———
O God, help me to ———
Share your feelings and responses with the group.

Chapter Three

Experience—
The Raw Material
for Doing Theology

Marge Adams is telling Walter about their son's problems. Needing his advice and support, she had broached the subject gingerly, describing David's poor showing in school, low motivation, breakup with his girl friend, and use of marijuana.

She had been fearful about Walter's reaction, but after a few sputterings about "that irresponsible kid" and "a lawbreaker under our roof," he settled down to discuss the matter with her. They need to decide how to handle his pot-smoking, how to deal with the school authorities and, perhaps most important, how to help David overcome his depression, develop incentive for finishing high school, and begin to plan for the future.

Because most of us face a family crisis like this at some time or other, it offers us a basis for looking at experience in terms of the raw material it provides for doing theology.

When *experience* was proposed by John Wesley and others as one of the guidelines for theological interpretation, they meant *Christian* experience, not *general* experience. They were referring to the experience of personal faith, assurance of salvation, witness of the Spirit, and communion of the saints. The experiences through which God makes himself known to us are primarily, in their view, prayer, worship, and Christian fellowship.

Our historical consciousness helps us understand, however, that this restriction of God's activity to the sacred, or spiritual, realm was the result of a Greek dualism, which consigned this world to the devil and sought escape in heaven with God.

This viewpoint has created generations of "heavenly minded people who were no earthly good," and thereby has removed the best, most conscientious people from active involvement in the struggle to shape this world according to God's plan. It also completely ignores the biblical understanding of God as the Lord of history, directly involved in everyday happenings. The data for doing theology come not just from high moments of prayer and worship, but also out of the ongoingness of life.

Any experience can be a religious experience. All that prevents it from being so is our blindness to the presence of God in it. The regular practice of making theological meaning out of our experience will help us transform ordinary events into meetings with God. Like Moses, we will be able to hear God speaking to us from a plain, ordinary bush and be led to take off our shoes, "for the place on which you are standing is holy ground" (Exod. 3:5).

Let us then look at the various aspects of everyday, general experience, illustrating them from the Adams family situation.

Needs

First, looking at experience from the inside, the initial motivating factor is need. Human needs are organized in pyramid fashion, with the organism concentrating first on meeting the most basic needs.[1]

To begin with, the body insists that enough food, clothing, and shelter be secured to insure physical *survival*. We can presume that, with a nourishing, home-cooked meal under their belts, none of the Adams are preoccupied with survival needs, and hence have turned their attention to those higher on the scale.

We next become concerned with *safety* and seek security, stability, protection, and freedom from fear and anxiety. We strive to establish structure, order, and limits in our environment. David, for example, is testing the limits set by his parents and the school authorities, but at the same time, subconsciously, he is asking them to enforce the rules. He is not ready yet to determine his own code of behavior and will feel more secure when firm limits can be mutually agreed upon.

Our next quest is for love, affection, and *belonging*. We feel the pain of rejection and loneliness and turn to

41

persons in general, and to family and friends in particular, to find caring relationships. David is seeking satisfaction for this need through relationships with friends, more than family, at this stage, and the recent breakup with his girl friend Cindy is a source of deep pain and disappointment. Marge's need for acceptance is met by her family and a group of close friends, and by participation in a deep fellowship at her church.

Our next need is for *self-esteem*, which is rooted both in our own sense of competence and achievement and in the appreciation and respect of others. We want to feel free, adequate, and strong. We need to experience accomplishment and mastery, and we look for attention and recognition from others. If our need for self-worth is met from both these sources, we feel good about ourselves. Otherwise, we experience feelings of inferiority, weakness, and discouragement. Because of his estrangement from Cindy, David is having these feelings now and needs support and encouragement. The need for self-esteem is crucial for his father also. At mid-life, Walter lacks the strength and energy he had ten years ago, finds his sexual appetite waning, and is starting to feel his age. Where he works, men of his age cannot expect many more promotions, and the responsibilities he carries are routine and unchallenging. He realizes that he has fewer years to live than he has already lived, and relationships with his family are becoming more complex. He tries to escape these concerns by pouring himself into his work, but the gnawing feelings of inadequacy and low self-esteem just won't go away.

Next we seek the freedom and resources for *self-actualization*, striving to fulfill our God-given talent and potential. Full expression of our gifts leads to a sense of fulfillment and inner peace. Without it, we feel restless and dissatisfied. Marge Adams' most pressing need is to develop her potential. She is frustrated because her artistic and executive abilities are going untapped. The realization that her life is slipping away, and that opportunities to express and develop these gifts will soon no longer be available, makes her somewhat irritable and unable to devote her whole being to her family.

Finally, we have the need for harmony and *unity* with the universe and with God. Even when all other needs are met, we still feel incomplete and discontented because, in the words of St. Augustine, "Thou hast made us for thyself, and our hearts are restless 'til they find their rest in thee." We strive to "put it all together"—to know, understand, and appreciate the whole creation and to be in harmony with it. We need to feel deeply confident that the universe is one, that it is God's, that we are at home in it, and that we are at peace with him.

All three of the Adams lack this sense of harmony. They are active members of the church, and even have attempted family worship. But God does not seem very real to them, and their lives are so divided and harried that they experience no deep sense of peace and serenity. They are not aware of God's presence in their current situation, nor does it occur to them to ask for divine guidance.

All our behavior, and hence all our experience, is motivated by one or more of these needs.

Feelings

Our success or failure in satisfying our needs generates a wide spectrum of feelings, which also play an important part in our experience.

When our survival needs are met, we feel basically comfortable; when they are not, we feel discomfort or pain. When our environment provides protection and stability, we feel safe and secure; when the limits are removed, when change comes too swiftly, when risk becomes high, or when guidance is unreliable, we become anxious and fearful. We feel loved and accepted in groups where we belong; when those around us do not express affection and caring, we feel rejected and lonely. Situations in which we receive attention and appreciation meet our need for self-esteem and help us feel adequate and important; we feel inferior if we fail to achieve or to receive recognition. Experiences of self-actualization help us to feel fulfilled; if our gifts are not utilized and our potential is not reached, we feel frustrated and depressed. When we "find our rest" in God and experience oneness with his creation, we feel whole and complete; separated from God, we feel alienated from ourselves, from other people, and from the universe.

The Adams are full of feelings. David wants to feel secure in his own decisions but still becomes anxious when he goes too far or makes a mistake. Right now he is feeling rejected and despondent because of Cindy. He has a sense of inferiority where studies are concerned and feels inadequate in personal relationships. He has not yet discovered his gifts and has no real sense of purpose or direction.

Walter feels loved by his wife and family. He is admired by his friends, but he still feels inferior and discouraged because of his lack of recognition and achievement at work. He is unfulfilled, not only because his potential is not being tapped in his job, but also because he has not sought other outlets for his gifts.

Marge finds her surroundings stable and dependable, and feels accepted and cared about by her family and friends. Occasionally she feels rejected and lonely when Walter spends more of his evenings at work than at home. She receives recognition and satisfaction from her work with Girl Scouts and in the choir at church. For years she has felt fulfilled as a homemaker, but lately she has become more troubled and depressed, with the gradual realization that household duties are demanding her best energies, while her creative talents remain largely undeveloped.

All three feel some alienation from God deep within themselves, though they attend church regularly and try to worship him as best they know how.

Intentions and Actions

Our feelings activate our intentions. We decide how we will go about meeting our needs. Then we implement our intentions, acting them out in quest of satisfaction.

We plant a garden, turn on the water tap, pull up the covers, or open a window, to meet our physical needs. We obey the speed limit, follow the doctor's orders, keep a daily schedule, or make a long-distance phone call, to insure stability and reduce anxiety. To meet our need for love and belonging, we flirt, get married, or join a club. To develop self-esteem, we brag, practice diligently, become a yes-person, or enter a contest. To become self-actualized, we change jobs, develop a hobby, or leave home. To discover harmony with God and nature, we attend church, go on a camping trip, or study Eastern religions.

David Adams is acting out his feelings of insecurity, rejection, and inferiority. His sullen attitude at home, failure to complete assignments, withdrawal from friends, and recourse to smoking pot—all are indications that his basic needs are not being met. His intention is to find a sense of security, acceptance, self-confidence, and fulfillment, but at this point he has no clear idea how to go about it. He is asking for help.

Walter's intention is to preserve what remains of his

45

self-respect. He has lost a great deal of confidence at work and does not want a failure with David to sap his esteem further. He will turn his anger and frustration against David if he is not helped to see what is happening. His intention is to use David to support his own sagging ego—to meet his own pressing need for self-esteem. Clearly, David and his father, each acting out of his own need, are on a collision course.

Marge may be able to keep her wits about her and, for the moment at least, subordinate her own need for self-actualization to the needs of the family. She does find her role in the family rewarding and is glad she can be a source of security, love, and appreciation for her husband and children. This function has met her needs for belonging and worth, but lately it has not satisfied her, and she is growing resentful of their inability to give her as much as she gives them. This episode with David may be the straw that breaks the camel's back. She may just explode, tell them all to "go to hell," and walk out.

Our intentions are translated into actions as we strive to meet our needs. That is experience as viewed from the inside.

But that is only half the story. For in acting to meet our needs, we encounter the outside world.

Outer Circumstances: Limits and Possibilities

Some external circumstances offer *possibilities* for meeting our needs, while others set *limitations*. Our environment is made up of the world of nature, the world of technology, the world of social organization, and the world of interpersonal relationships. The limits and possibilities of our experience come from all these sources. We are affected by the realm of plants and animals, air, soil, and water—the world in which we live and breathe. We have available a whole range of man-made tools, from the teaspoon to the computer, which help to determine what we can or cannot do to meet our needs. Social structures—laws, governments, customs, languages—also shape our life.

But the point at which our experience is most powerfully influenced from without is in our relationships with other people. These offer both limits to, and possibilities for, the ways we carry out our intentions for meeting our needs.

Our relationships with *family* set the basic patterns for all other relationships with both *peers* and *authority figures*. We have friends, co-workers, and acquaintances with whom we associate. And we have teachers, employers, supervisors, and others whom we perceive to be more powerful, important, wise, or good than we are. We tend to relate to peers as we did to our brothers and sisters, and to authority figures as we did to our parents.

These limits and possibilities are evident in the Adams' situation. Some of the environmental factors are natural—the atmosphere, the climate, and the rich farm belt in which they live. Others are technological—their home, car, telephone, and banking privileges. Still others are offered by their culture—the words they use as they talk together, the expectation of their social class that David will go to college, the sex roles that have led Walter to become the breadwinner and Marge the homemaker, and the social mobility that has them living more than a thousand miles from their parental home.

But the most significant elements influencing the Adams family are personal. David resents the limits his parents place on his freedom. He has the opportunity to go to college, but this now seems more like a limitation on his future. His father's busyness restricts his accessibility, so that David often has no understanding man to talk with about his self-doubt and future plans. His mother's accepting nature makes her easy to talk to. But he increasingly finds her overprotective and demanding, which limits his sense of autonomy, and this makes him angry.

David's current poor performance and emotional depression are a threat to his father's sense of adequacy. It would be a severe blow to Walter's already deflated ego if his son flunked out of school or had to see a psychiatrist. On the other hand, he just may have the skill and composure to be supportive and helpful as his son works through an adolescent crisis. David's problem offers Walter the possibility of proving his adequacy as a father.

Walter's wife and daughters also offer both limits and possibilities. Without family obligations, he would be free to quit his job and look elsewhere. But Sarah and Janet will be his financial responsibility for another ten years, so he can't afford even to think about changing jobs. However, life with Marge has been rewarding. Her warmth and enthusiasm have helped him to become aware of his feelings. She and their children continually call forth his best. They offer support, solace, and stimulation when he comes home from a dull, frustrating day at the office.

Marge Adams realizes that, after all, she is still David's mother. The choice she made years ago to marry and have children is a commitment she cannot back out of now. To be sure, she often feels hemmed in by the constant demands of her family. David's current erratic behavior and Walter's job dissatisfaction and moodiness concern her deeply, and the girls soon will be in adolescence. But there are real possibilities for growth and self-actualization in keeping faith with her commitments. Marge will continue to develop her gifts for empathy and home management. And after the girls are in junior high, she will have more time for art, volunteer activities, and perhaps even a part-time job.

The authority figures in the Adams' environment are the high school principal, the police and courts, and the upper-level management in Walter's company. They set limits for what David must do to stay in school, what he ought not do to stay out of trouble, and what Walter must do to keep his job and obtain a promotion. But they also offer opportunities—the gateway for David into a rewarding future and encouragement to live responsibly, and the means for Walter to make a social contribution, support his family, and witness to his faith among his co-workers. They also remind Marge of her expected role as a woman, and of both the limits and possibilities this affords.

The Adams' friends are also involved. It was Cindy who precipitated the crisis by breaking off her relationship with David because he kept insisting that they sleep together. This caused feelings of guilt, anger, and rejection in David, and he is subconsciously taking energy away from school and family to work these through. His other school friends tried to cheer him up by offering him a "joint," but this only contributed further to his present difficulties.

The trust level at Walter's office is too low for him to share his dissatisfaction with his colleagues. This limitation on help from that source has led him to look elsewhere for friends to whom he can express his feelings. Fortunately, he and Marge are in a sharing group at church, which meets every other week for Bible study, prayer, and sharing of personal concerns. They have talked freely about job frustrations, but it will be difficult to share something as personal as David's current problem. However, Walter is feeling enough pressure that he intends to bring it up at the next meeting, in the hope of gaining support, understanding, and some group wisdom as to possible solutions.

This group is also a main source of support for Marge. She and the other women have shared their feelings about being trapped in the homemaker role, and she is sure they will keep confidential whatever they are told about David's situation. The Adams also are fortunate to have a pastor who gives the impression of being a fellow pilgrim rather than a religious authority, so Marge feels free to talk over her problems with her, as well. In fact, if they cannot resolve things in tonight's family conference, she plans to ask the pastor to meet with the three of them to help them understand one another better, sort out their feelings, examine their options, and make some decisions. Other people tend to provide possibilities, rather than limitations, for Marge, perhaps because she is such an open person herself.

Activity of God

We have looked at our experience in terms of both inner processes and outer circumstances. To limit our analysis to those factors, however, is to ignore the activity of God. For the Spirit of God is involved in every aspect of our experience.

The Bible emphasizes the presence of God *with* us much more than his distance *from* us. The illustrations given here are suggestive of how God continues to act in our life—meeting our needs, identifying with our feelings, guiding our intentions and actions, and presenting limits and possibilities through other persons and external events.

It is God's plan that we have needs and that they be met. God's Spirit is actively meeting them through our experience. Jesus came that we "may have life, and have it abundantly" (John 10:10). Abundant life is life in which all our needs are being met. We use the expression "salvation," or "becoming whole," to talk about how God meets all our basic needs.

God provided quail and manna in the wilderness (Exod. 16:13-18), and Jesus fed the hungry five thousand out of compassion (Mark 6:34, 44). God gives sun and rain to both the evil and the good (Matt. 5:45), and Jesus discourages anxiety about survival by pointing to God's care for the birds and lilies (Matt. 5:25-33). The Ten Commandments provide structure and limits for our life, and Jesus offers guidance for finding stability in his parable of the wise man who built his house on the rock (Matt. 7:24-27). God meets our needs for *survival* and *security* in these and many other ways.

Ruth found acceptance and *belonging* in the family of her mother-in-law, Naomi, enabling her to say, "Your people shall be my people, and your God my God" (Ruth 1:16b). The early disciples experienced the love of Jesus, who would "lay down his life for his friends" (John 15:13), and were commanded to "love one another; even as I have loved you" (John 13:34). After his death, they found belonging, as "they devoted themselves to the apostles' teaching and fellowship" (Acts 2:42) and admonished each other, "If God so loved us, we also ought to love one another" (I John 4:11). God and the church likewise meet our need for love today.

Men and women of faith receive praise and recognition for their righteousness (Heb. 11). The dignity and worth of all people are assured by God, as declared by the psalmist: "Thou hast made him little less than God, and dost crown him with glory and honor" (Ps. 8:5). Through accepting Zacchaeus (Luke 19:1-9) and the woman at the well (John 4:7-29), Jesus helped them gain a new sense of *self-esteem*. He does the same for us.

Paul described his *self-fulfillment* in these terms: "I have fought the good fight, I have finished the race, I have kept the faith. Henceforth there is laid up for me the crown of righteousness" (II Tim. 4:7,8). The Bible speaks of self-actualization as being "set free from . . . bondage . . . and obtain[ing] the glorious liberty of the children of God" (Rom. 8:21) and as being "born of the Spirit" (John 3:8b). This same experience is available to us in Christ.

Although the emphasis in the creation story is on subduing and having dominion over the earth, and does set human beings, as servants of God, over and apart from the rest of creation, the Bible also stresses our harmony with nature. This is found in the book of Job: "For you shall be in league with the stones of the field, and the beasts of the field shall be at peace with you" (5:23); in Isaiah's vision: "The wolf shall dwell with the lamb . . . and a little child shall lead them" (11:6); and in Paul's comprehensive understanding of the redemptive work of Christ: "In him all things were created, in heaven and on earth . . . in him all things hold together . . . for in him . . . God was pleased to dwell, and through him to reconcile to himself all things" (Col. 1:16-20). *Unity*, reconciliation, reunion with God, is a major theme throughout the Bible. Jeremiah speaks of it in terms of a new covenant: "I will put my law within them, and I will write it upon their hearts; and I will be their God, and they shall be my people" (31:33b). The parable of the prodigal son offers an irresistable image of the desire of God to be united with his people. This experience of unity and harmony he offers to us.

God is no stranger to *feelings*. He knows our whole range of emotions, because "in him we live and move and have our being" (Acts 17:28).

In the Old Testament, God is pictured as feeling anger (Exod. 4:14; Isa. 34:2), wrath (II Kings 22:13; Ps. 90:7), hatred (Isa. 1:14; Amos 5:21), sorrow and grief (Gen. 6:6, 7), displeasure (Ps. 2:5; 60:1), jealousy (Exod. 20:5; Zeph.

52

1:18), pity (Joel 2:18), compassion (Ps. 78:38; Mic. 7:19), steadfast love (Exod. 34:6, 7; Lam. 3:22), love (Hos. 11:1-4; Jer. 31:3), delight (Deut. 1:15), pleasure (I Chron. 29:17), patience (Jer. 15:15), and rejoicing (Isa. 65:19).

In the person of his son Jesus Christ, God felt pain inflicted by Pilate's soldiers, fear in the garden, rejection at the last supper, discouragement over Jerusalem, impatience with the disciples, and loneliness on the cross. On the other hand, he also knew the pleasure of a wedding feast, the security of a carpenter's home, the love of an understanding mother and loyal followers, a sense of achievement from healing and teaching, a feeling of fulfillment in being faithful, and a sense of wholeness through serving as the means of reconciling the world to himself.

The feelings of the people of the Bible range from the pleasures of those in King Solomon's courts to the pain of those in defeat and exile. Moses felt both the security of his mother's care in Pharaoh's household and the later anxiety of confronting the Pharaoh with the demand, "Let my people go." Isaiah was fully accepted in King Uzziah's highest councils, whereas the prophet Jeremiah was rejected and cast into a pit to die. Nicodemus, as a member of the Sanhedrin, certainly felt important and respected by others, while Zacchaeus, being small of stature, expressed his feelings of inferiority by becoming a tax collector, so he could lord it over others. Stephen's sermon (Acts 7) reveals how fulfilled he felt through knowing and doing God's will. Jonah, however, became very apprehensive and depressed when he resisted God's command to go and preach in Nineveh. The feeling of wholeness and completion came to Paul on the Damascus Road, while the rich young ruler went away still alienated and lost. Even as God understood and accepted this wide range of feelings, so he does ours.

God also inspires and guides our intentions and actions. He called Moses to lead the Hebrews out of bondage and toward the land of milk and honey. He sent out Abraham, who did not know where he was going, to find the "place which he was to receive as an inheritance" (Heb. 11:8). He says to the weary of soul and body, "Come to me . . . and I will give you rest" (Matt. 11:28). In response to our quest for meaning, he promises to "guide you into all the truth" (John 16:13). He calls us to deny lesser needs in order to satisfy the greater ones (Matt. 16:24).

The activity of God also is readily perceived in the limits and possibilities of outer circumstances. He led Israel through the desert by means of a pillar of cloud and fire (Exod. 13:21, 22), yet he prevented Moses from crossing over into Canaan (Deut. 32:48-52). He promises eternal life, but reminds us that if we become disciples of Jesus, "Foxes have holes, and birds of the air have nests; but the Son of man has nowhere to lay his head" (Luke 9:58). And his son Christ Jesus, "though he was in the form of God . . . emptied himself, taking the form of a servant . . . and became obedient unto death . . . on a cross" (Phil. 2:6-8). The infinite possibility of divinity became the mortal limitation of humanity.

The Bible also tells how God acts in our experience through *people*—whether they are *family*, *fellow pilgrims*, or *persons in authority*.

He saved the baby Moses for his life of destiny through the action of his sister and mother (Exod. 2:1-10). The forgiving attitude of the prophet Hosea toward his wayward wife mirrors God's acceptance and forbearance toward all his people. He taught the sons of Jacob a lesson in penitence and reconciliation through the magnanimous attitude of their brother Joseph (Gen. 43-45).

In the New Testament, God chose to show aspects of the faithful life through ordinary people. It was Peter,

54

sometimes impetuous, sometimes cowardly, who first recognized Jesus as the Messiah (Luke 9:20). The gift of two pennies by a poor widow exemplified unselfish generosity (Luke 21:1-4). A "woman of the city" anointed Jesus' "feet with her tears" (Luke 7:36-50). A converted slave named Onesimus ministered to Paul in prison.

God also makes himself known through persons who wield power and authority. He goaded Israel into revolution to win their freedom from slavery by hardening the heart of Pharaoh. He blessed his people through faithful kings like Hezekiah and Josiah, and punished their unfaithfulness through the invasion of the Assyrian, Sennacherib, "the rod of my anger" (Isa. 10:5). And he called them to repentance and righteous living through prophets like Nathan, Amos, and Isaiah. Jesus himself "taught them as one who had authority, and not as their scribes" (Matt. 7:29).

In our experience today, just as in biblical times, God is at work to accomplish his purpose of bringing peace and goodwill to all people (Luke 2:14). He operates through our needs, feelings, intentions, and actions, and makes use of other people to challenge us with limits and possibilities.

We can discover what God is likely to be doing with the Adams family by examining what we know of his nature through his self-revelation in the Bible and in Jesus Christ.

God is the *loving Parent.* As the father accepted both the wayward prodigal and the self-righteous elder brother, so does God understand and accept the despair and loneliness of David Adams, the anger and self-depreciation of Walter, and the discontent and resentment of Marge. He wants to reconcile this family to one another, and to himself, and enable them to achieve family harmony, inner peace, and a sense of active involvement in his struggle to redeem the whole world.

God is the *righteous Judge*. He expects faithful obedience and responsible behavor and is grieved when people cut themselves off from him by rejecting his standards and ignoring his grace. The Adams are confronted by this holy God. David has cut himself off from both Cindy and his parents by his self-indulgent behavior. Walter is alienated from himself, his family, and his work because he has sought satisfaction and self-respect through the false gods of success and status, rather than through service and witness. Marge's present feelings of unfulfillment are the result of her early choice of marriage over college and career. They all are implicated, whether they recognize it or not, in an unjust and oppressive society that maintains its wasteful living standard by consuming irreplaceable resources and by exploiting laborers in Third World countries.

God is the *creative Leader*. His creation is ongoing, and he constantly reminds us: "Behold, I am doing a new thing; now it springs forth, do you not perceive it?" (Isa. 43:19). He wants to help Marge Adams utilize her creative potential in painting and pottery, perhaps through opening a small ceramics shop. He wants to release Walter's creative energies both at work and through an avocation, perhaps gardening. He wants to lead David to discover and develop his gifts in a constructive, service-oriented career. And he wants to guide them all into a redemptive relationship with one another, the world, and himself.

In theologizing about our experience, therefore, the basic question has to do with God's activity. We ask, What is God trying to accomplish in this situation? What is God doing here? What is God trying to say to me through this experience? What response is God calling me to make?

It may be that, when the Adams reflect theologically on

their current experience, they will discover still other ways God is working in their lives. And in order to do this ourselves, we now turn to some practical ways of using the data from our experience in doing our own theology.

TO DO IN PRIVATE

This exercise, called "Anatomy of an Experience," is designed for writing in your journal.

Relax, close your eyes, and let your mind run over the significant recent experiences in your life. Recall how they came about, what the circumstances were, who was involved, and how you responded.

Focus on one of those experiences. Let your mind linger over details, such as the place where it happened, how people looked, what they said, and how you felt. Concentrate on your own behavior. Did you initiate, or react? Did you act impulsively, or think things through? Were you angry, frightened, loving, or elated? How do you feel about the episode now?

Now take up your pen and begin writing. Use the following format:

1. *Describe.* Write down as much of the experience as you can remember. Record both the external event and your inner feelings and responses. Take as long as you wish, but a brief, succinct paragraph will do.

2. *Analyze.* Recall the several aspects of the experience outlined in this chapter as you reflect on yours.

    a. Needs. What needs were you striving to meet through that experience?

    b. Feelings. How did you feel in that situation? How did you express these feelings? Were others aware of how you felt? Did you want them to be?

    c. Intentions. What were you trying to accomplish? How did you communicate your intentions? Did others know what you were trying to do?

     d. Actions. What did you actually do? Were your actions consistent with your intentions? Did they result in meeting your needs? In retrospect, would other behavior have been more appropriate?

     e. Other People. Who was involved with you? What did they do and say? How did they affect you and shape the experience? Did they act as a limitation or a possibility?

  3. *Theologize.* What was God's part in that experience? What was he doing? Were you aware of his presence at the time? Can you see it now? Toward what goal was he working? What did he want for you? From you? If this is difficult, ask God to help you. Pray that he will show you what he wants you to learn from that experience.

  4. *Personalize.* What does that experience say about the kind of person you are? Make a list of adjectives that describe you as you appeared in that situation.

  Now look at your list. How do you feel about this portrait of you? What might God want you to do about the person who emerges here?

  You have been "praying with your pen." Whether you phrased it that way or not, you have been in conversation with God. What you have written reflects his thoughts, as well as yours. Now close your reflection by thanking him for his guidance in helping you "do theology."

TO DO IN A GROUP

  If you have all done the "Anatomy of an Experience" exercise, proceed directly to sharing your journal reflections. Take turns reading them aloud, with the group receiving and responding to each experience with understanding and respect. Make it clear that members need not share unless they want to. Allow enough time to deal with each person until the group feels a sense of completion, and until that person is ready to move on.

If your group is large, divide into subgroups, but reassemble at the end of the session to share feelings and impressions. Perhaps each subgroup could tell one significant interchange that highlighted their time together.

If group members have not done the individual journal work, or prefer a fresh exercise, use "Limits and Possibilities." Write the steps on the blackboard to save time in explaining the procedure.

Begin with a period of quiet meditation in which you relax, close your eyes, and think over recent events in your lives. Recall what has been happening, who has been involved, and how you have been feeling.

Next, write endings to the following sentences in your journals. Each is given in two forms: in one, you address yourself; the other asks you to surmise what God might be saying to you. Use whichever feels most natural. Complete each one in light of your reflection on recent experience.

1. *I am the kind of person who* ———

   or

   _____(your name)_____ *, you are the kind of person who* ———

2. *The biblical image with which I identify right now is* ———

   or

   _____(your name)_____ *, you are like the biblical image of* ———

   (If the appropriate image does not come readily to mind, the collage on page 61 may stimulate your memory and imagination.)

3. *I want to become* ———

   or

   _____(your name)_____ *, I am calling you to become* ———

4. *The limits and possibilities in my situation are:*

Possibilities	Limits
(1)	(1)
(2)	(2)
(3)	(3)
	or

_____(your name)_____ *, I am saying yes to some things, and no to other things in your life:*

Yes	No
(1)	(1)
(2)	(2)
(3)	(3)

5. *My next step is* ———

or

_____(your name)_____ *, I want you to* ———

When everyone has finished writing, begin the sharing process, following the procedure outlined in the last exercise. Be sure people feel free to share just as much as they want and no more. Keep one another mindful that God is acting and speaking through both limits and possibilities. Ask: What is God saying yes and no to? What is God calling you to be and to do in your situation? How is he wanting to love, judge, and guide you?

Spend a few moments looking over the next chapter and making suggestions about the exercises and the leaders for the next session. Close with prayer, with members expressing thanks to God for his presence in this session and asking

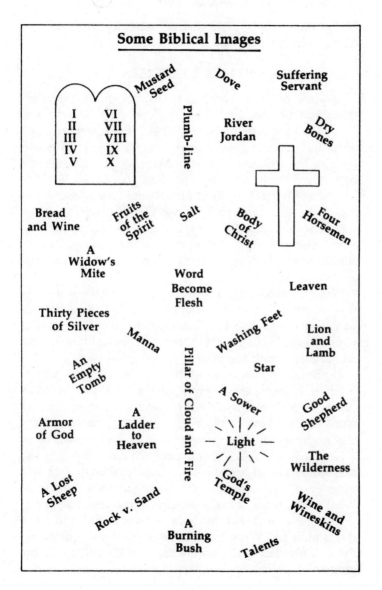

Some Biblical Images

Mustard Seed

Dove

Suffering Servant

I II III IV V VI VII VIII IX X

Plumb-line

River Jordan

Dry Bones

Bread and Wine

Fruits of the Spirit

Salt

Body of Christ

Four Horsemen

A Widow's Mite

Word Become Flesh

Leaven

Thirty Pieces of Silver

Manna

Washing Feet

Lion and Lamb

An Empty Tomb

Pillar of Cloud and Fire

Star

A Sower

Good Shepherd

Armor of God

A Ladder to Heaven

Light

The Wilderness

A Lost Sheep

Rock v. Sand

God's Temple

A Burning Bush

Talents

Wine and Wineskins

his guidance in the theological reflection you will be doing between now and the next meeting.

OTHER EXERCISES

In place of or in addition to the foregoing exercises, these may be used.

1. "Walking Around in the Bible." Try to experience a scriptural event in your imagination. Close your eyes and imagine that you are there—for example, at the encounter between Joseph and his brothers (Gen. 43-45), the conversation between Ruth and Naomi (Ruth 1:6-18), the call of the disciples (Matt. 4:18-22), or the healing of the Gerasene demoniac (Mark 5). Observe what happens, talk with those involved, let your imagination place you in the situation, and talk with the Lord about how the event is affecting you.

Write an account of the scene as you visualize it. Use the "Anatomy of an Experience" format to analyze this imagined happening. Let God speak to you at the level of your needs, feelings, intentions, and/or actions in this scene. Share with the group.

2. "Simile." Pick a word that identifies you—father, teacher, homemaker, jogger, farmer, traveler, or some other. Complete this sentence, putting your identifying word in the blank: *Being a* _____ *is like* ——— Use an image or descriptive phrase in your sentence.

Now ask yourself: What experience has led me to use this simile? What are the limits and possibilities in this experience? How might God be acting and speaking in it? What simile would I like to be able to use about myself in this connection? What needs to be done in order to make this simile fit? Write your answers to these questions, then share your reflections with another person or the group.

Chapter Four

Reason—The Process of Meaning-Making

No event or experience has meaning in and of itself. The structure in a situation, the causality in a series of events, the size, shape, and color of an object, as well as the religious significance of an experience, are all meanings we assign.[1] If a sunset is beautiful, it is because we think it is. If a room is small, it is because we perceive it as smaller than other rooms we have been in. If the other side started the war, it is because we so interpret it. If our church decides to send our building fund to support Mother Theresa in Calcutta, it is because our understanding of the Bible and faithful discipleship suggests that we do so.

Others may see the sunset as ordinary, the room as large, the war as our fault, and a new sanctuary as more important than Mother Theresa. It may disturb us to realize this, but we can have no absolute assurance that our meanings are right and the others wrong. We do not have access to a set of certain principles to direct our thinking, or infallible rules to guide our decisions. We must figure things out for ourselves.

This does not mean, however, that every idea is as good as every other one. Nor does it suggest that we are at liberty to live as we please or to believe what we wish—not if we are Christians. For we are accountable to the four guidelines. We must test our thoughts, choices, and acts against the Bible, Christian teaching, rational principles, and the wisdom of our own experience.

This process of interpreting experience as a basis for decision and action, we call meaning-making. It may be illustrated in a diagram.[2]

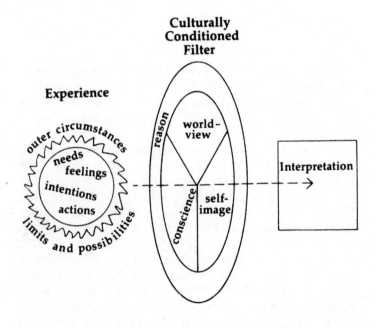

The raw data of experience, generated by our needs, feelings, intentions, actions, and outer circumstances, are organized into an interpretation by passing through our "spectacles." This culturally conditioned filter has four parts. The rim is called reason, and the lens is trifocal, made up of our particular world-view, our conscience, and our self-image. The box labeled interpretation bears little resemblance to either the complex experience or the interpretive filter. It is neat, orderly, and manageable, but a limited and inadequate version of the original. Let us examine each aspect of this meaning-making filter.

Reason

The rim of the spectacles represents reason, our ability to think and draw conclusions. This sets the boundaries within which meaning-making must take place. We have to use the reasoning abilities God has given us. Nothing, not even the revelation of God, can bypass our eyes and ears, our memory and imagination, our perception and logic, in our comprehension and interpretation of an event or idea.

We see and hear something. We correlate these sensations with similar messages which have been previously stored. We identify the size, shape, loudness, goodness, and cause-and-effect relationships of the various elements in the experience. We call forth past experience from our memory, pictures from our imagination, word meanings from our concept bank, and associations from our previous practice with analysis and synthesis. On the basis of all this, we determine that the hamburger is too salty, the prayer too long, the skirt too short, or that we will resist a temptation because our "body is a temple of the Holy Spirit" (I Cor. 6:19).

That is a very brief, unscientific explanation of what actually happens, but it helps us see the complexity of the meaning-making process and how much we depend on our rational faculties to make sense from our experience. The processes of sensation, perception, conceptualization, memory, imagination, logic, analysis, and synthesis all help us translate the raw data of our experience into a system of thought. Of course, a lot is lost in the translation, but life would be intolerable if we were constantly encountering a jumbled mass of need messages, feeling tones, uncoordinated intentions, conflicting actions, and flashing yes and no signals from outside. Of necessity, we ignore most of these stimuli, so that what does pass through the filter will provide an orderly basis for thinking and choosing.

It is important that the information passing through the filter is the kind we want our ideas and actions shaped by, and that the messages we neglect are of less consequence to us. This is the function of the three aspects of our spectacles—our world-view, conscience, and self-image.

World-View

Our world-view is shaped largely by the way life is explained to us as children. We learn that stoves are hot and ice is cold, that yards are safe and streets are dangerous, that dinner comes at noon and supper at night (or lunch at noon and dinner at night). We discover green grass, blue sky, and brown, red, or black earth. We encounter love, conflict, crime, and peace. We identify the difference between friend and foe, day and night, simple and complicated. From sharing a Bible story, we may mistakenly conclude that "King Solomon must have been fond of animals, because he had many wives and one thousand porcupines."[3] We locate God up in heaven and the devil down in hell.

As we mature, of course, our world-view changes. We

become less subject to what others tell us and better able to pick and choose for ourselves. But just as a fish thinks the whole universe is water, so it is hard for us to escape the conditioning of our culture and to adopt a view from outside. Social pressure urges us to accept current notions.

We can adopt a Christian world-view, however, and fill this section of our spectacles with biblical images and theological themes. We need not let our view of life be wholly conditioned by the headlines, TV commercials, and our eighth-grade civics class. Nor must we let the Twenty-third Psalm, the annual Easter sermon, and the Christmas pageant be the sole sources of our Christian consciousness. We can be intentional about what makes up our world-view. We can gather the material we want to use in doing our own theology.

Words are important to our world-view. The way we name the things in our world is significant. What we learn, or decide, to call things influences how we see them. Our vocabulary reflects what we believe about our world. For some the policeman is Officer Friendly; for others he is a "pig." Our sobbing parents complain about God having "taken Grandma away," and as adult Christians, we still labor under the misapprehension that God causes cancer.

So in doing theology we must pay close attention to the words we use and the meanings we attach to them. We ask one another, What did you mean by that? or, Give an example, please. We make use of commentaries, Bible dictionaries, and theological word books to get at original and varied meanings of words.[4] It is important for clear communication that we share common understandings of the words we use. Our Christian community will remain superficial as long as "atonement" means "rescue from a wrathful God" to some of us and "at-one-ment" to others, or "repentance" is seen as "changing direction" to some and as "self-abasement" to others.

The content of our world-view helps to shape the "box" that results when we interpret our experience.

Conscience

Our values and notions of right and wrong are shaped also by our childhood upbringing. Whether we understand an experience to be good or bad, affirming or guilt-producing, is a function of the conscience element in our spectacles.

The content of our conscience, for the most part, comes from our culture by way of parents and teachers. We are taught that sex is dirty, that nice boys don't throw stones, that it's OK to steal if you don't get caught, or that we should do as we are told. We learn that it is all right to shoot people on TV, or when we are in a uniform, or with play guns, but not otherwise. We discover that men open doors for ladies and that women don't swear in public. We notice and remember that it is good to help some people, bad to befriend others, right to save money and wrong to spend it (or vice versa), praiseworthy to tell the unwelcome caller that mother is not home, but disgraceful to help a fellow student during an exam.

The devices through which these standards of conduct are imparted to us are reward, punishment, and the example of our elders. When we violate the injunctions thus approved or condemned, we feel guilty; when we follow them, we feel OK about ourselves.

Although culture shapes our conscience, as we mature, we become better able to choose our values, standards, and models. We can adopt our own rules and determine the best sources for guidance. For Christians the four guidelines become an important resource. We turn to the Bible and Christian teaching to enrich or replace inadequate patterns and principles. The "be not anxious" advice of Jesus might supplant the achievement drive learned from hard-working parents. We might discover that the body is beautiful and that sex is a joy, through a careful rereading of the creation story. Jesus' attitude toward outcasts and Peter's vision in Acts 10 might help us to see people of different colors, views, and life-styles as interesting and attractive, rather than as enemies or rejects.

When we examine the precepts that have guided our behavior, and we discover their sources, we are freed to determine whether we want to follow these guidelines, or others. The Bible, historic examples of Christian witness, and current views on Christian ethics can point us to new content for our conscience, by which decisions and interpretations can be informed and tested.

Self-Image

A third aspect of our culturally conditioned filter is the way we perceive ourselves. From our earliest awareness we receive messages that we are cute, smart, clumsy, or careless. We are better athletes than our brothers, slower readers than our sisters, or better looking than the girls next door. The way others react and relate to us and the feedback we get from our appearance and performance shape our self-image, influencing our behavior and limiting or expanding our potential.

Our self-perception is affected also by the groups we belong to. The way in which a social group or class understands itself and the way it is seen by others may be inaccurate and biased. But these views still make an impact on its members' image of themselves. Certain behavior is expected of a college graduate, a divorcee, or a slum-dweller. Different life-styles are exhibited by a Korean immigrant, a Midwestern farmer, and a Pueblo Indian. A

Presbyterian, a Pentecostal, and a Jew have dissimilar patterns of worship and religious training.

Group identity shapes personal identity. If we grow up on farms, we think of ourselves as farmers. If most kids in our school go on to college, we consider ourselves college-bound. If ours is a church-going town, we go to church too. If people in our church wave their hands and go to the altar to be saved, then we probably will do that too. We see ourselves as the kind of persons our families nurture us to be, our social group expects us to be, and those on the outside perceive us to be.

Of course, we can change this self-image as we grow older. We can leave our group or class and enter another, adopting the identity it offers us. We can decide not to go to college, and we can become plumbers. We can move out of an ethnic neighborhood into an upper-middle-class suburb. We can reject the "loser" image that has been fixed on us and adopt a positive, hopeful attitude. We can desert our posh social set and join a commune.

Having chosen the self-image of committed Christians, we strive to fix that identity firmly in our spectacles so that it will influence the way we view ourselves and our experience. We may turn to the personages of the Bible, the biographies of great Christians, and our faith community, for guidance in forming our identity. The biblical persons and characteristics found in the "I Am" collage on page 72 may suggest qualities we would like to imitate or change. We may wish to identify with Martin Luther, proclaiming "Here I stand," or Susanna Wesley, praying with her children, or William Wilberforce, combating slavery. We may find in the courage and devotion of members of our own congregation the stimulus we need to make our self-image more consistent with that of a faithful disciple.

The more we self-consciously integrate elements of our

Christian heritage into our self-image, the more we will experience ourselves that way and act out of that identity.

Interpretation

When we use our rational faculties to explain what has happened to us in the process of meeting our needs, we are strongly influenced by the way we view life, understand right and wrong, and see ourselves. The resulting interpretation of our experience is as accurate as our words can make it, but it is influenced by the world-view, conscience, and self-image we have acquired, or chosen.

Much of the experience is filtered out by our limited spectacles, so that one person's interpretation is likely to be different from that of others. It requires sensitivity and patience to try to understand how the spectacles of another have influenced his or her interpretation, so that genuine communication or "shared meaning" can take place.[5] The meaning I make from an experience may be quite different from yours. The way to come to a mutual understanding is not for me to impose my interpretation on you, or vice versa. Instead, we must share our meanings with each other so that we both know why and how we come to the views we hold. Shared meaning, or the understanding of what we each feel and believe, and why, is much more important than agreement.

This is what Jesus meant when he said, "By this all . . . will know that you are my disciples, if you have love for one another" (John 13:35). Love is caring enough about others to respect their right to be different from us, and to make the effort to understand what makes them different. The Christian church, therefore, is a community of diversity, in which persons are enriched by difference, free

71

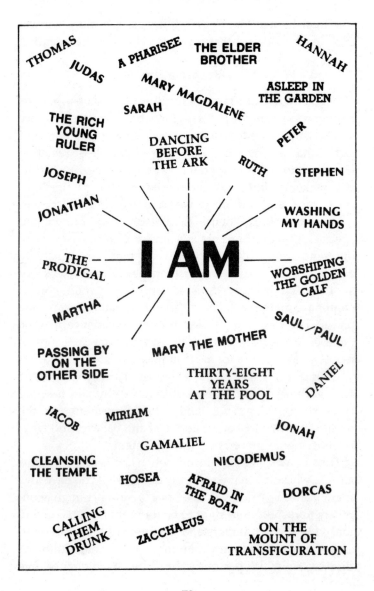

to disagree, and united by acceptance, understanding, and shared meaning.

Meaning-Making in the Adams Family

We now look at how this process might work in the Adams family conference. The three of them are seated at the kitchen table, drinking hot chocolate.

They all make use of the rational tools in the rim of their spectacles—their capacity to receive sensations, make associations, utilize concepts, call back memories, draw conclusions, imagine possibilities—the ability to take a problem apart into its various elements and reconstruct it in a new form.

Walter's world-view is shaped by a lifetime in business. He thinks in terms of profit and loss, productivity and competition, manager/employee: family conflict must be managed; David must become a productive citizen; the family should be run on standard procedures; every organization has a boss. His conscience tells him that smoking marijuana is wrong because it is illegal, that children should obey their parents, and that David should go to college and be "successful." He perceives the situation out of his own self-image as a lower-echelon corporation executive who has never quite made it. From his perspective, the problem will be solved if David becomes more assertive, goes to college, does his homework, and stops smoking pot.

Marge views the situation from the standpoint of relationships and personal fulfillment—for all three of them. Her value system emphasizes service to others, sensitivity to feelings, and success, in terms of being where you want to be and doing what you enjoy. She sees herself as a caring person who sacrifices self for others but who is seeking greater self-actualization. She wants David to accept himself as a person who can make mistakes and feel uncertain and still be OK, to seek reconciliation with Cindy, and to graduate from high school, to keep future options open while continuing his search for direction. She would like to see Walter either accept his limitations, make the best of his present situation, and develop some hobbies, or else quit his job and look for another. For herself, she wants less family responsibility and more time for her painting and ceramics.

David's beliefs have been much like those of his parents until recently, when he has begun to think more for himself. He is questioning his father's view of success, resisting his mother's suffocating concern, and wondering whether his too-readily assumed identity as college-bound, law-abiding, and "straight," is what he really wants. But the filter his parents and culture have given him is still very much a part of him. So he feels guilty about arguing with Cindy, failing his exams, breaking the law, and not living up to his parents' ideals. He knows he ought to apologize to Cindy, catch up on his school work, apply to college, and start speaking to people again. But these choices will not fully satisfy him, for they will still reflect his parents' spectacles. He won't find much real self-respect, inner peace, or fulfillment until he develops his own.

So because each of them is wearing different spectacles, each puts a different interpretation on the problem and seeks a different outcome. They must therefore try to understand one another's perspectives in order to discover shared meaning and reach a mutually agreeable solution. It remains to be seen whether they will be able to develop the insight and empathy to understand one another, or whether they will need help from someone else to achieve a breakthrough to shared meaning.

Let us leave the Adams for a while and turn to our own meaning-making procedures.

TO DO IN PRIVATE

Prepare to write in your journal. This exercise is called "Chapters."[6] Read through these instructions before beginning. Then get comfortable, close your eyes, and let your mind drift back over your entire life. Don't write anything yet. Just let images flit in and out—faces, happenings, familiar places, objects. Let your feelings flow; don't try to control what comes into your thoughts. Picture your mind as a screen with a multi-media show going on. You see familiar scenes and people; you hear the voices of loved ones and associates. The emotions you felt at memorable moments come over you again.

Now the torrent of images gradually subsides, and your mind begins to focus on a few key turning points in your life. It is as though the pages of a book have been whirring past your eyes, and now as the pace slows, you begin to see the chapter titles. Those are the times when you made an important decision, when a critical event occurred, when your life changed course. As those "chapters" come to mind, open your eyes and list them. A few words or a phrase will identify the event. After you have listed ten or twelve such turning points, arrange them in chronological order.

Next, study your list and pick out one "chapter" to explore in depth. Name it, and write the title at the top of a fresh page in your journal. Work back through the meaning-making diagram, examining your interpretation of this event and how it has been shaped by your spectacles. Finally, consider how your interpetation might change if you were to introduce specifically Christian content into your filter. Write brief responses to each of the following:

1. *Interpretation.* What meaning does this event have to you now? What difference has it made in your life since it took place? Why did you choose this as a significant turning point?

2. *Culturally Conditioned Filter*.
   a. *World-View*. How have the beliefs you have acquired shaped your view of this "chapter"? And of life itself as mirrored in it?
   b. *Conscience*. Was this a good or a bad experience for you? Was your behavior right or wrong? What causes you to say so? What factors have shaped the conscience out of which you were operating?
   c. *Self-Image*. Who are you as reflected in this event? What in your background has led you to view yourself this way?

3. *Christian "Spectacles."* What theological theme or Biblical image best characterizes this "chapter" in your life? What specifically Christian content might you introduce into your filter to throw new light on it?
   a. *World-View*. How did you encounter God in this "chapter"?
   b. *Conscience*. How did your decision and behavior contribute to God's purpose in the world? How did you aid the increase of love and justice? The enhancement of personhood? The building of world community?
   c *Self-Image*. With what character in the Christian story do you most identify in this experience? How does this image help you understand yourself and your responsibilities better?

If you do not have time to answer all these questions, reflect on question 3. Close by thanking God for this and all the "chapters" in your life, for his guidance in the past, and for his promise to lead you into the future.

TO DO IN A GROUP

To use the "Chapters" exercise as the basis for this session, each person should have a blank sheet of paper, with several boxes of crayons available.

Turn your paper sideways and fold it into three equal sections. From your list of "chapters," choose three that represent significant turning points and that you are willing to share. Illustrate with crayons the meaning these experiences have had for you. Use no words, but let color, shape, and design communicate the meaning. Make three drawings, one for each "chapter," one on each panel of your paper. This is not an art contest, so don't worry about how your drawings will look.

When everyone is finished, take turns sharing the pictures. As each person holds up his or her drawing, the members should receive it by saying what they see, how it makes them feel, and what they think was happening in that chapter. Then it is the presenter's turn to describe what he or she was trying to communicate. Be sure each member has a chance to share.

If your group is large, divide into fours. One of the listeners in each subgroup will focus on the world-view reflected in the "chapters," the second on conscience, and the third on self-image. The listeners should watch for elements in the presenter's existing spectacles, and also should introduce biblical images and theological themes. Similar listening assignments may be made if the group does not divide.

An alternative experience is the journal exercise, "Dialogue With My Job."[7] Close your eyes and think about your work—either your employment or what you consider your main responsibility. It may help to personify the job in the form of a boss or some other person who represents its demands and challenges. Write a conversation with your job, with you speaking first and the job replying. Let the dialogue flow as it will; do not try to control or direct it. One part of you will be dialoguing with another part. Just listen in and write down what they say.

When the dialogue has run its course, go back and reread it. Write brief responses to each of these questions:

1. What world-view did the job represent? What contrasting beliefs did I express? Where do I really stand on these issues?

2. Was my conscience represented by me or by my job? What am I telling myself to do in my work? Where do these injunctions come from? Do I really want to follow them?

3. What self-image does my job express? Does the other side of me reflect a different self-understanding? Where does each image come from? Which do I like best?

4. What biblical image, theme, or character speaks to me out of this reflection?

5. What might God be saying to me and to my job? What does he want me to do in this situation?

Either share in the total group or divide into groups of four, using the procedure previously outlined. If there is time, each member can read his or her dialogue aloud and then summarize responses to the five questions. If not, each can share (1) the issues that emerged in the dialogue, (2) insights or learnings gained, and (3) a biblical theme or image that throws new light on his or her work-life.

When all have shared, close with "popcorn prayers"— offer one-word responses to each of the following:

In regard to my job, Lord, I thank you for ———
In my work, Father, I ask your forgiveness for ———
Oh God, in my job help me to ———
Father, in my work save me from ———
Lord, as I return to work tomorrow, help me to ———
Amen.

Before the group departs, spend a few moments looking at chapter 5, so that you understand what you are to do before the next session. Be sure to bring your Bibles next time.

OTHER EXERCISES

For further reflection along this line, use these exercises.[8]

1. "My Fall from Grace". Recall the time in your life when you first lost your innocence—your first experience with lying, disillusionment—with feeling ashamed, or inadequate. Live this over in your mind, and write it out. Remember what it was like to encounter the serpent, eat the forbidden fruit, realize you were naked, and hear God call out, "Where are you?" (Gen. 3).

Ask yourself what aspects of world-view, conscience, and self-image shaped your understanding of that event at the time. How do these influence your interpretation of it now? How has God been active both in this experience and in your growing understanding of it? Share in the group.

2. "My Restoration". Follow this same process in reconstructing and reflecting on an experience in which you were found by grace—a time when you felt accepted, whole, united with your roots, blessed. Recall how it felt to see the Lord "high and lifted up" (Isa. 6:1), to see the burning bush (Exod. 3:2), to have the scales fall from your eyes (Acts 9:18), to have your sins forgiven (Mark 2:5), or to have the Lord invite himself to your house for supper (Luke 19:5). Let yourself feel now the way you did then. Ask God for a new gift of grace, another restoration.

What beliefs, moral standards, and self-perceptions best help you interpret these experiences of restoration? Write your reflections, then share them with another person and the group.

Chapter Five

Scripture—
An Object of Faith
or a Resource for Faith?

The Apostles' Creed does not mention the Bible. Apparently, in early times the Scriptures were seen only as a resource to nourish faith and not as an object to believe in. The Bible is our guide, not our straitjacket.

Scripture has primacy among the four guidelines for doing theology. If a belief or interpretation proves contrary to Scripture, it does not belong in a Christian's faith. If, because of the influence of "the American dream," or the ethics of advertising, or my parents' opinion of me, I attach a meaning to my experience that I later discover runs counter to biblical teaching, then I would do well to rethink it.

The appropriate way to use the Bible in faith translation is as a resource for guiding and testing our meanings, and not as a prop for an interpretation we already have decided upon. Paradoxically, persons who revere the Bible as a holy book containing the sacred words of God also tend to use it for proof-texting. They believe that every word of Scripture literally has been inspired by God and is in the Bible in just the place and the way that God intended. Or they affirm the "plenary inspiration" of the Bible, meaning that all its ideas have their source in the mind of God. Like everyone else, however, such persons wear spectacles which cause them to select or emphasize those passages or themes that fit in with and reinforce their own predetermined views. Hence, while accepting the Bible as the revealed word of God, being human, they read it through their own culturally conditioned filters.

But the view of Scripture as the infallible word of God is only one among several approaches to the authority of the Bible. Some see it as containing God's word—as a human record of the form in which God's revelation has been perceived by people. Others describe it as a source book, containing guidelines for faith and life, rooted in the past, but still relevant today.

Another view is that the Bible records the history of God's people. God has revealed himself in events—from creation, through the cross, to the founding of the church. Through understanding this story, we can come to know God and his word and will for today. In the reading of this historical record of the interaction between God and his people, his Spirit invites us to enter a growing and confronting relationship with him in the here and now.[1]

Each of these views represents the way some Christians understand the Bible. The viewpoint underlying this book is spelled out in the previous paragraph. But whatever notion we have of the origin, authority, and validity of the Bible and its relevance for our lives, we need some guidelines for interpreting it. We want to avoid proof-texting, which is simply using scripture to support our own biases. Rather, we want to get at the meaning the Bible had for those who originally developed it, and to discover and appropriate the message God has in it for us. And we want to be sure that this meaning and message is as reliable and accurate as possible.

Interpreting the Bible

We now examine some principles and a process of biblical interpretation that will help us use Scripture as a resource for doing theology. In the accompanying diagram,[2] biblical interpretation is depicted as an "event in me," bringing together "my situation" and what was intended by the words of the Bible. Each is set in its respective context and must be so understood. The words of a passage must be seen in the light of the surrounding paragraphs, the book in which they appear, and the type of literature in which they are found. They must be tested against the major themes of the Bible and can be understood only in terms of the life-world of Bible times.

Similarly, the context from which we come affects our interpretation. We read the Bible with spectacles shaped by our contemporary world. The persistent life concerns that prompt our basic questions and intentions also profoundly influence the attitude we bring to the Bible. Our church experience, too, affects our interpretation.

The Spirit of God is involved with us as we read his word. He has messages of comfort, challenge, forgiveness, judgment, or guidance to convey. Our primary purpose in reading the Bible is not for its literary value or to become familiar with Hebrew history, but to receive these messages.

We will look at these principles one at a time.

1. *Try to understand the life-world out of which the passage comes.* This involves some study of the historical background of both the times in which the events occurred and the time in which the passage was written. When we

Interpreting Scripture

understand the Jews' resentment against the Romans and their strong loyalty to God, for example, it becomes apparent that when Jesus said, "Render to Caesar the things that are Caesar's and to God the things that are God's" (Luke 20:25), he was not putting those two obligations on a par, for a faithful Jew owed nothing to Caesar.

The characteristics of the biblical life-world do not just leap out at us from the printed page. To learn historical background, we must study some Bible helps. Archeologists, linguists, and Bible scholars have spent their lives gathering historical information to help us interpret Scripture. It may be found in commentaries, Bible handbooks, atlases, Bible dictionaries, and histories and introductions to the Old and New Testaments.[3]

2. *Relate parts to the whole.* Although the Bible is made up of sixty-six books, many of which are composites put together by an editor, it is also *one* Book with a coordinated message, a related cast of characters, and

a continuity of development in the story of a people. Any passage we read must be correlated with the overall story and the message of the Bible as a whole.

This involves, first of all, interpreting verses in relation to their immediate context. The well-known verse from Amos, "But let justice roll down like waters, and righteousness like an everflowing stream" (5:24), sounds majestic but vague when heard alone. But when read in the context of surrounding verses that condemn those who "trample upon the poor" (5:11), "afflict the righteous, . . . take a bribe, and turn aside the needy in the gate" (5:12), it becomes apparent that Amos is calling his people to repentance for gaining wealth through exploitation of the poor.

Second, we need to interpret Bible passages in light of the overall message and purpose of the book where they appear. For example, the book of Hosea was written to call Israel to repentance for falling away from the worship of God and making offerings to the false god Baal. In this context it makes sense for Hosea to use his personal experience with his unfaithful wife, Gomer, to illustrate how God will forgive and accept his people back, if they will but repent.

Third, words and passages must be understood in terms of their meaning at the time they were written. When a given word has more than one possible interpretation, the context and line of thought of the author help us determine which was intended. Paul, for instance, uses the word "circumcision" as a symbol of the attitude that substitutes outward form or custom for an inner experience of faith. Hence, his words (Rom. 2:25-29), though grounded in the historical situation when some Christians were requiring Gentile converts to be circumcised, are relevant to any age. The basic meaning of his statement, "Real circumcision is a matter of the heart," is neither that we should take a knife and trim the heart muscle, nor that faith is superior to being circumcised, but that the mark of a true Christian is an inner experience with Christ and not an external form of religious practice or belief.

A fourth aspect of the scriptural context is the type of literature in which the passage is found. The biblical writers used poetry, saga, legal code, geneology, proverb, letter, historical narrative, and drama; each type has a particular style, vocabulary, structure, and content. In our day we have different expectations of a novel, a poem, a magazine article, and a business letter. Similarly, in the Bible we do not expect a drama such as Job to be historically factual, a series of legal documents (Leviticus, for instance) to be entertaining, or a love song like the Song of Solomon to observe the prudish niceties of a prayer in church. It is particularly helpful to recognize that the book of Jonah is a short story, not a historical narrative, which frees us to discover its deep missionary significance, rather than worrying about whether its hero actually was swallowed by a big fish.

Finally, in weighing the Bible's value and usefulness in faith translation, consideration of context leads us to relate any passage, story, or single book to the overall message. On this principle, the books of Esther, Song of Solomon, Ecclesiastes, and James have been viewed by some interpreters as conveying messages less important than, or even contrary to, the central idea of the gospel. The psalms that call for vengeance against enemies have been eliminated from the Psalter by some churches. Sermons are seldom heard about the Hebrews thinking that God wanted them to slaughter their enemies (Deut. 32:39-42) or about Paul's teaching that a woman should keep silent in church (I Tim. 2:12). Although these are all in the Bible, they are clearly not in harmony with its basic teachings and hence do not provide valid content for our spectacles in making theological meaning out of our experience.[4]

3. *Look for unifying themes.* The overall message of the Bible is like a tapestry composed of major and minor threads. It contains an amazing amount of theological pluralism, with teachings and emphases of different periods, and writers at variance and even in conflict with one another. Examples of major clashes are the opposing views of prophets and priests in the Old Testament, the conflicting viewpoints on Gentile converts expressed at the Jerusalem Council (Acts 15), and the contrasting emphases on faith and works by Paul and James. But there are a number of principal themes running throughout the Scriptures that tie together the various books, ages, and emphases.

These themes are foundation stones upon which a framework for interpreting the Bible may be built. Various passages and stories may be measured against them, and they test our own interpretations of life and experience, as well. If we think that God has caused a calamity in our life, or that we have committed the unpardonable sin, we must ask whether our understandings would be consistent with the major scriptural teachings.

Here is a starter list of some of these key threads in the biblical tapestry. This list is neither complete nor authoritative. As you read the Bible, you and your group are encouraged to reword the list, add themes and references, and cross off any you do not find to be central and unifying.

Some Biblical Themes

The Initiative of God—Judgment and Love (Heb. 12:5-6; Hos. 11:1-4; Isa. 10:1-19; I John 4:7-11)

Jesus Christ—Son of Man and Son of God (Rom. 8:3; Gal. 4:4; Phil. 2:5-11; John 1:1-14)

Creation and the Fall (Gen. 1–3; Job 38; Pss. 100:3, 102:25; 104:24-30; Isa. 43:18-19; Rom. 5:12-14)

Human Nature—Image of God and Sinfulness (Gen. 1:27; Eccles. 7:29; Rom. 3:23; James 3:9; II Peter 1:4)

Death and Resurrection (John 11:25-26–12:24; Rom. 6:1-11; 5:15-17; I Cor. 15; Mark 15:24–16:20)

Sin and Salvation—Alienation and Reconciliation (Mark 2:17; Luke 15:11-32; 23:34; Acts 2:38; Eph. 2:8)

Exodus–Canaan–Exile–Return (Deut. 6:21-23; 8:11-20; II Kings 17:22-23; Ps. 137:1-6; Isa. 65:17-25)

The Covenant—Made, Broken, Renewed (Exod. 19:4-6; Ps. 78; Jer. 7:23, 31:31; Ezek. 16:59-60; Heb. 9:15)

Bondage—Liberation (Exod. 13:3, 20:2; Deut. 15:15; Isa. 61:1-2; Jer. 30:8; Rom. 7:15–8:2; 8:21; Gal. 5:1)

Freedom and Responsibility (I Cor. 7:22-23; John 8:36; I John 3:16-18; Gal. 5:13-15; Rom. 6)

The New Birth (John 3:1-8; II Cor. 5:17; I Peter 1:3; I John 4:7)

The Cross—Redemptive Suffering (Isa. 53; Matt. 27:27-54; I Cor. 1:18; Heb. 9:14; 12:2)

Servanthood (Matt. 20:25-28; 23:11; Phil. 2:1-8; Rom. 12; I Cor. 9:19-23; 13; John 12:26; 13:3-17)

Discipleship (Matt. 4:19, 10:24; Mark 8:34-38; Luke 14:33; John 13:34-35; 15:1-17)

Faith (Heb. 11:1–12:2; Luke 7:50; Rom. 1:17; 3:28; 5:1; Gal. 2:16; Eph. 2:8)

A Pilgrim People (Exod. 13:18-22; Num. 10:29-36; Luke 9:57-62; 13:22; Heb. 11:8-10, 11:13-16)

The Church—the Body of Christ (Rom. 12:4-8; I Cor. 12; Eph. 4:4-16; John 17)

The Kingdom of God—Already and Not Yet (Matt. 4:17; 13:24-52; Luke 17:20-21; John 18:36; Rev. 11:15)

Shalom—Justice, Peace, Wholeness, Well-Being, Abundant Life for All People (Isa. 2:4; 11:3-9, 32:1-4, 15-20; Amos 5:24; Mic. 4:3-4; Matt. 5:3-12; John 10:10; 14:27; Col. 1:15-20; Eph. 1:3-10; 2:13-22)

The Last Judgment (Matt. 25:31-46; 24:3-51; Mark 13; Rom. 14:10-12; Heb. 9:27-28; Rev. 14)

Eternal Life (John 6:40; 14:1-3; 17:2-3; Rom. 6:23; I Cor. 15:51-56; I John 2:17; 5:11-12)

4. *Try to identify the intentionality of the text.* The people—storytellers, writers, editors—who were responsible for any passage being in the Bible had a reason for including it. What were they trying to say? God has something he wants to communicate through this passage. What does he want us to hear?

All the study we have done thus far—on historical background, literary context, and unifying themes—is essential to discovering the intentionality of the text. However, we have reference not only to that time of writing, but to this time of reading. So another set of questions is required. What is the situation at this time, to which this passage might speak? What are people in today's church saying and doing about the issues the passage refers to? What fundamental life questions are people asking today, to which it might be a response? What questions do I want to address to this passage? What is God trying to say to me through it?

These questions lead us into the next set of guidelines. For not only do we need to examine the Bible, but we must let it examine us as well.

5. *Become familiar with the contemporary life-world.* We need to know the characteristics of our cultural situation as we interact with the Bible. What is our prevailing world-view? Value system? Image of humanity? What present-day thought-forms, life-styles, social movements, and political and economic structures are most influential? Who are our heroes and heroines? What makes us feel proud or guilty?

What slogans, fashions, films, songs are popular? What ethnic group, economic class, national background, religious tradition, and generation do we come from? What hurts are we feeling? What issues are we facing? What sins should we be confessing? What dreams are beckoning us?

These factors in our consciousness influence the questions we ask of the Bible, the interpretations we give to it, and the responses we make.

6. *Be aware of our persistent life concerns.* There are certain questions all people ask at some time in their life. We may discover some of these by simply translating our basic needs into questions. How can I ensure my survival? How can I find security and protection? How can I experience love and affection? How can I win esteem? How can I find fulfillment? How can I discover harmony in the universe and with God?

You or your group may wish to make your own list of persistent life concerns. What are the basic issues of your life that demand explanation or resolution? Here is a starter list for your consideration:

Who am I?

How can I know I am loved?

What is the purpose of my life?

To what cause shall I give my life?

How will I know that my life counts?

How can I know right from wrong?

How can I be really free?

How can I make the world a better place?

What does my promise mean?

What is the meaning of my pain?

What will happen to me when I die?

Are the consequences of my actions dependable?

Does it matter how I live?

How can I find persons to love and to be loved by?

What's the use?

These are questions we bring to the Bible. They will influence the meaning a passage has for us. If a particular story or chapter does not seem to address any of these concerns, we well may dismiss it as outdated or irrelevant. But when we read it another time, it may come alive with meaning. A concern that formerly was dormant is now pressing for resolution. The passage addresses it. God speaks in response to our question, an event takes place, and we become a different person.

Bible study requires an alertness to our persistent life concerns. When these intersect with the message of the Bible, we find a faith-meaning in our experience. We are doing theology.

7. *Stay involved in the church.* "No prophecy of scripture is a matter of one's own interpretation" (II Peter 1:20). Bible study is basically a group process. We must be mutually accountable within the covenant community. We need to rely on the insights, knowledge, and experience of other Christians to enrich and evaluate our individual interpretations. Sermons, church school classes, study groups, informal conversations, symbols, stained-glass windows— all can provide assistance to us in doing theology with the help of Scripture.

8. *Consider our current life situation.* What is going on in my life right now? What decisions am I facing? What disappointments have I had? What wounds need healing? What victories am I celebrating? What projects and relationships am I working on? What books am I reading? How is it with my family? My health? My job? Can I balance my budget? Am I sleeping well at night?

These may not be ultimate concerns, but we bring them to our reading of the Bible, nevertheless, and they affect the meaning we find in it. A key question to ask of any Bible story is, Is this my story? We want to know how the Bible relates to our present problem. We are looking for guidance, understanding, or forgiveness. So when a phrase or image pops out at us, we "latch onto" it. And why not? The God who is concerned about the hairs of our head and the sparrows that fall (Matt. 10:29-31) also cares about our worries, choices, and upset stomach.

The danger in this approach is that we can be misled easily. When we are consciously looking for verses to speak to our condition, our subconscious mind, or mere chance, may lead us in faulty directions. We will be protected from such misinterpretations, however, if we make use of the other guidelines to check the validity of the messages we think we are receiving.

9. *Expect God to speak and act.* The inspiration of the Bible is as available to the reader as it was to the writer. When we come in an attitude of prayer and seeking, God is with us as we read his Word. When the intentionality of the text encounters our life situation, sparks fly. A biblical theme speaks to a persistent life concern. We find ourselves in the experience of a character in Scripture. A Bible story becomes our story.

Perhaps light bulbs flash and sirens blow. Perhaps we hear the still small voice. Our heart sings, our palms grow sweaty, we get a sinking feeling in our stomach, or our eyes fill with tears. The signals may vary, but we know that God has spoken to us through his Word.

We discover in the story of Gamaliel (Acts 5:33-42), for example, that God also can use a cautious fence-sitter to accomplish his purpose. We encounter the theme of servanthood in Isaiah, chapter 53, and are reminded that our life takes on purpose through service to others. In response to our need for love and acceptance, we hear the familiar words, "For God so loved the world . . . " (John 3:16). God is active in these events of insight, forgiveness, comfort, and direction. As we read the Bible we can expect him to be there. We can expect things to happen to us.

91

10. *Be ready to respond.* We also can expect God to ask us to do something in response to his Word. We must be prepared to change. Since Scripture is a record of God's mighty acts with and through his people, we can anticipate that he will want to move history through us, as well. Our interpretation of Scripture must be concrete in terms of the action expected of us right now.

Of course, these directions will need to be tested against the other principles of interpretation. But faith translation leads to decision and action. God may ask us to encourage a friend or forgive an enemy. He may call us to change our vocation or accept a difficult assignment. He may challenge us to give sacrificially or to oppose an injustice. The key question to ask is, How must my life become different when I begin to take this passage seriously? And then act on his answer!

The Adams Find Themselves in the Bible

The Adams family is probably not ready for this thorough an approach to Bible study. They are Bible-believing people, however, and are receptive to God's word in a sermon or church school class, on a TV program, or in a discussion with their pastor or sharing group. But suppose they do decide to make serious use of Scripture as a resource for their life. What are they likely to find?

Walter may discover in the story of David and Absalom (II Sam. 13:1–19:8) a parallel to his experience of estrangement from his own son. Upon reading it he well might exclaim, "This story is my story—or could be!" He might decide then that it is more important for him to try to understand his son's pain and indecision than to protect his own pride by insisting that "father knows best."

Walter also may find in Nicodemus (John 3:1-10) a

92

parallel of his own mid-life crisis. For he is experiencing a similar gnawing doubt, wondering, Is this all there is? and asking whether he can be "born anew" at his age. He may be ready, for the first time in his life, to really hear the words of Jesus, "Unless one is born of water and the Spirit, he cannot enter the kingdom of God." The image of the light on the lampstand (Matt. 5:14-16) may summon him to see his work as an opportunity for witness. The biblical theme of creation may encourage him to find outlets for his creative potential in both work and leisure-time pursuits. Or he may hear, in the parable of the sower (Luke 8:5-8), the question, What kind of soil are you?

For Marge Adams, the Scriptures turn up an entirely different set of images and insights. She senses the new wine of her aspiring liberation to be bursting the old wineskin of her role as housewife and mother (Matt. 9:17). Like Ruth of old, she had left her family and hometown to follow her husband to his place of work, saying in effect, "Where you go I will go, and where you lodge I will lodge" (1:16). But increasingly she is feeling uprooted and separated from her kinfolk, culture, and childhood locale. She has faithfully fulfilled the scriptural description of a good woman—one who "looks well to the ways of her household, and does not eat the bread of idleness" (Prov. 31:27). Yet she does not experience often the promise of the next verse—"Her children rise up and call her blessed; her husband also, and he praises her" (31:28). Rather, she sometimes feels used and taken for granted.

While early in their marriage she had adhered to the scriptural injunction, "Wives, be submissive to your husbands" (I Peter 3:1), she now finds Paul's words, "Christ has set us free; stand fast therefore, and do not submit again to a yoke of slavery" (Gal. 5:1), more appealing. She is convinced that for her, abundant life

(John 10:10) must involve the opportunity to express and develop her God-given talents and to use them in her church "to equip the saints for the work of ministry, for building up the body of Christ" (Eph. 4:12).

Marge sees her relationship with her son to be like that of the father with the prodigal (Luke 15:11-24)—giving David the freedom to make his own choices, even when she believes him mistaken, but always being willing to listen, accept, and try to understand. It is painful to see him hurt himself this way—even as it must have been to that other parent, and as it must be to God—but she knows it is the only way for him to grow, mature, and take responsibility for his own life.

David well may identify with the despondent words of Job, "The thing that I fear comes upon me . . . I am not at ease . . . but trouble comes" (3:25, 26). In the transition from adolescence to young adulthood, he is experiencing the biblical theme of death and resurrection; but although he feels the passing of the carefree dependence of youth, he as yet has had hardly a clue as to what the resurrection of adulthood will bring. He needs to hear the biblical word—without the cross, there can be no resurrection; "unless a grain of wheat falls into the earth and dies, it remains alone; but if it dies, it bears much fruit" (John 12:24). With some important decisions facing him, he may hear the challenge of Joshua, "Choose this day whom you will serve" (24:15).

In his relationship with Cindy, David can identify with the feelings of Jacob, who, knowing he had wronged his brother Esau, was afraid to return and face him (Gen. 32). Similarly, David does not know how to approach Cindy and may need to struggle with God as Jacob did (Gen. 32:24-32), in order to see the face of God in the face of his friend (33:10) and treat her accordingly. The theme of alienation and reconciliation is present in all his relationships, and he needs to follow Jesus' suggestion—when "your brother has something against you, . . . go; first be reconciled to your brother" (Matt. 5:23, 24).

As they can help the Adams, so the Scriptures can help us translate our faith into present circumstances. To assist us in this, we now turn to some structured exercises for using the principles of biblical interpretation in doing our own theology.

TO DO IN PRIVATE

Choose a Bible passage or story you think will be meaningful. The many passages mentioned in this and previous chapters, the list of biblical themes, and the collages of biblical images and personages included earlier will help in selecting one. Assistance also may be gained from a topical concordance, which lists passages by themes, or by thumbing through The Bible in Today's English Version (the Good News Bible) or another version that divides the chapters into sections with descriptive titles, thus calling to mind a familiar story or important idea.

First, paraphrase your passage. Write it out in your own words, substituting parallel images and experiences out of your life-world. The purpose of the paraphrase is to discover the message for you and your situation in the passage and to put it into words you and others cannot fail to understand.

Next, study your passage in light of the diagram on page 83 and the description of the process of interpreting Scripture. Make use of Bible helps, such as a commentary, handbook, introduction, dictionary, and word book, if available.[5] But also draw on your own previous Bible knowledge and good common sense. Reading the paragraphs before and after the passage will also provide some clues. Write brief answers to these questions:

1. What are some characteristics of the *biblical life-world* out of which this passage comes?

2. What is the *context* of this passage? What are its key words, type of literature, and relation to the message of the Bible as a whole?

3. What is its major *theme*?

4. What is its *intentionality* or basic message?

5. To what in your *contemporary life-world* might this passage be speaking?

6. To which of your *persistent life concerns* does it make a response?

7. How might others in the *church* interpret it?

8. To what in your personal *life situation* might its message be relevant?

9. What might *God be saying* to you through it?

10. What is he calling you to do, or be, in *response?*

If time is short, choose the most helpful of the questions, or limit yourself to these two.

1. What is the basic message of this passage?

2. How would your life change, if you took its meaning seriously?

Close your meditation with a brief prayer, thanking God for the insight, guidance, or conviction he has given you and asking him to strengthen you to carry out the challenge he has placed on your heart.

TO DO IN A GROUP

Begin this session by reviewing the principles of biblical interpretation. Then move to a time of sharing, telling the passages studied and learnings gained. If your group is large or time is limited, divide into subgroups of three. While one person is sharing, the other two may take the listening roles of the biblical "prophet" and "priest." The prophet assumes the stance of "Thus saith the Lord," confronting the speaker with his or her needs and shortcomings. The priest expresses the attitude of "Come unto the Lord" and offers the speaker understanding, comfort, and support. After one has shared, the roles are switched until each person has had a turn at all three.

Then reassemble and talk about what happened in the subgroups. Lift up ideas, highlights, and problems with interpretation, drawing on the resources of the larger group.

If your group prefers a different exercise, use this one called "Find Yourself in the Bible."[6] Each member looks through the Bible and chooses a character, parable, or chapter that speaks meaningfully to him or her. If this seems too difficult, you can all work with the same passage. For example, the description of the stoning of Stephen (Acts 7:55–8:8) contains a variety of characters with whom different people can identify.

Write these steps for individual study on a chalkboard or newsprint to have them before you as you work.

1. Read through the passage carefully.

2. Clarify the setting and context: Identify as many characteristics as you can of the biblical life-world (historical background, social situation, related events, movements, and persons involved) and the context (surrounding paragraphs, book, key words, and relation to the overall biblical message).

3. Identify the intentionality of the text: Write the key idea or central message in one sentence.

4. Who are you in this story? With which character, aspect, attitude, or idea do you identify?

5. What is the Good News for you in this story? What is God saying to you, whether by way of comfort, call to repentance, forgiveness, guidance, or challenge?

6. Give a name or title to the story.

When all have finished writing, begin the sharing. If time is limited, tell only the passage you chose, where you found yourself, the good news you heard, and the title you assigned. To give more time, break into threes and use the "prophet" and "priest" roles, returning to the larger group for a summary sharing.

For the closing worship, mention the learnings, insights, or questions God has given you through Scripture in this session. After each person speaks, the group might respond with, "Thanks be to God."

Read through the communion service before the next session, and bring copies of your last communion bulletin to the meeting.

OTHER EXERCISES

1. "Biblical Images." Select and reflect on an image from the collage in chapter 3—"light," for example (Luke 11:33; Matt.5:14-16). We are called to be a light for others, to point the way to meaning, purpose, and a relationship with God. Examine your life and witness in terms of this image. Recall a person who illuminated your life or thought. What did he or she do that brought you new insight? What direction does this suggest for your life-style? What are the sources of new light for you? What have you learned from them lately? How can you share these learnings with others?

Write responses to these questions, then share with the group. Take a similar approach in reflecting on other biblical images.

2. "Experiential Bible Study."[7] Select a passage that has meaning for you or for your group. Write out your own "translation" of it in words that you use when you feel, think, decide. Now let your translation encounter your

own experience. Ask: What is the underlying truth about life that is breaking through here? Where do I see it working in my life? What new possibility is God offering me? What person or situation do I see differently in its light? What concern or passion does it awaken in me? To what new cause or direction does it beckon me? Write your responses in your journal.

Now, in small groups of three or four, receive each person's translation. Listen for God's message coming to you through the others' filters. When all have shared, try for a consensus on the major thrust of the passage. Finally, back in the total group, share the core meanings and special insights that have emerged in the small groups.

Chapter Six

Tradition—
Dead or Alive?

The word "tradition" is not a very exciting one for many of us. We think primarily in terms of the present and future and do not want to be limited by the past. We view tradition as out-of-date, irrelevant, and confining. It seems dead and useless.

The tradition we speak of here, however, is "the dynamic, ongoing process by which the past becomes present and is carried into the future."[1] It is the accumulation of vital expressions of faith and responses to the living God, which forms an active connection between past, present, and future. Tradition is not primarily a body of knowledge, of belief, or of custom, to be preserved and transmitted from one generation to the next. Rather, it is the living process by which a culture or religious group understands itself and the events that shape its identity and life-style. In the words from *Fiddler on the Roof*, "because of our traditions, everyone knows who he is and what God expects him to do."

It is not so much limiting as it is freeing to be grounded in a tradition. Because we have our roots firmly planted in the soil of tradition, we are free to grow, branch out, blossom, and bear fruit.

As a family, for example, we have traditions for celebrating birthdays, sharing the household chores, and making decisions. When these things arise, familiar procedures go into operation, and we bake a cake, put a note on the refrigerator, or call a meeting. We belong to a family and are secure in its tradition. We act out of this identity and are free to fulfill ourselves within it. We are also free, as we mature, to move beyond it—to establish a new identity, join a different tradition, and put down new roots. But this is only because the dynamic quality of tradition enables us to carry it over and transform it in a new context.

As Christians, we also belong to a living tradition. We trust in a God of power and love, worship weekly in a particular manner, practice justice, and witness, because of who we know ourselves to be within this tradition. Our Christian tradition is not dead and static, but growing and changing. It is both stable and dynamic, because it is rooted in a God who is the foundation of the universe and who is also the power who moves in history to establish a kingdom "on earth as it is in heaven."

The word "tradition," as used in the church, has three meanings, which may be distinguished as "Tradition," "the traditions," and the "traditioning" process. These phrasings describe tradition in its authoritative, historical, and dynamic senses, which are depicted in the tree diagram on page 102.

The trunk of the tree represents Tradition in the *authoritative* sense. This is the living, self-renewing Word of God, who discloses himself anew to each age and setting. As revealed to and through the people of Israel

101

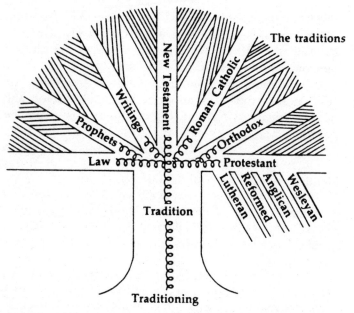

and through Jesus and his followers, it is recorded in, but not confined to, the Bible. The Tradition is the spring, out of which flows a never-ending succession of traditions. In the Old Testament, the Law (Genesis, Exodus, Leviticus, Numbers, Deuteronomy), the Writings (Job, Psalms, Proverbs, Ecclesiastes, Song of Solomon), and the Prophets (all the rest), represent three different forms of tradition or interpretation—each created in response to the life-giving Word. The various Gospels and letters in the New Testament also embody Tradition in differing strands, or traditions.

As a body needs clothes, so Tradition never appears to the human eye except as wrapped in one of the traditions. The wrapping when first formed is fresh, colorful, and inviting, but as conditions change, cultures vary, and people develop other needs and ways of expression, it no

102

longer communicates the kernel of Tradition effectively. The Word of God becomes obscured, rather than revealed, by the form of a particular tradition. Hence, a "re-form" is needed, which often produces a new tradition.

Already begun in the Old and New Testaments, this chain of formed and reformed traditions continued with the church fathers, the early creeds, the Roman Catholic, Orthodox, and Protestant branches of the church, and countless other efforts to do theology, down through the centuries. This is the *historical* meaning of tradition. God's people have been continually engaged in a creative effort to respond to the Tradition by developing traditions, the branches and twigs of the tree. As they made meaning out of experience in the light of Scripture, they developed a whole series of doctrines, symbols, catechisms, hymns, liturgies, forms of architecture, and organizational structures. Because all these have been influenced by their cultural spectacles and historical circumstances, new wrappings are repeatedly needed in order to clothe the Tradition faithfully.

The impetus for re-forming the traditions comes from tradition in the *dynamic* sense—the ongoing interaction of God's Word with God's people. This is represented by the spiral line that extends from the base of the tree into all its branches. In this "traditioning" process, the Tradition is translated into traditions relevant to particular times and places. Through this process the grace and power of God in Christ, which are at the heart of both Tradition and the traditions, are continually made known in new forms of expression, patterns of common life, and doctrinal formulations, in response to new needs and circumstances. In the words of James Russell Lowell's hymn,

New occasions teach new duties,
Time makes ancient good uncouth;
They must upward still and onward,
Who would keep abreast of truth.

From one perspective, the traditioning process is the activity of God's Spirit—judging the incompleteness of particular traditions, creating vital new expressions of the Tradition, and calling us to respond in ways that are both faithful and innovative. From the human standpoint, on the other hand, this process may be termed enculturation. Families and religious communities, striving to initiate their young into a vital experience of faith, endeavor to present the Tradition in contemporary, relevant, and appealing ways. In the process, two things happen. Individuals develop a sense of identity through commitment and through belonging to a community. And the church renews and reformulates its faith and way of life, while remaining faithful to its origins and commitments.

For example, a teacher is trying to help a confirmation class understand the kingdom of God. He asks each young person to think of an area of life and then to fantasize what it would be like if that area were directed fully by God. Each person writes a scenario of what would go on in their areas if God were in charge. Each then draws a picture on newsprint, illustrating the scenario, heading it "God at the Controls of———." On Sunday these newsprints are hung in the sanctuary like banners, and the subject of the sermon is "God at the Controls." Excerpts from the scenarios are read. Both youth and adults get a new slant on an old concept. Although we have never lived in a kingdom, we can understand that a vehicle or appliance works best when all parts respond quickly and efficiently to the touch of the operator. The kingdom of God is present when persons and situations are responsive to the touch of the Operator.

A new tradition has been established in this congregation. The traditioning process has been at work, and the Tradition is revealed in a new wrapping. The youth have been enculturated into a significant aspect of their faith, and the church has re-formed its tradition. Faith translation has taken place as these young people have led the church in doing their own theology.

This incident is only a small wrinkle in the long historical process of tradition, which has been transforming the wrappings of our faith for centuries, and continues at an even faster pace today. All the past interpretations or traditions have become part of our spectacles as we make meaning from our experience today. But the meaning we come up with also will be influenced by the beliefs, values, and prevailing self-image we have acquired from our particular group or subculture. The forms of worship, ethical standards, religious art and music, and beliefs that we emphasize will vary, because the spectacles through which we receive Tradition will filter it through in different forms and hues.

This is not only inevitable, but desirable, for if the Tradition is to be understood and internalized in our religious community, it must be clothed in garments we can relate to. As at Pentecost, we each need to "hear them speaking in his own language" (Acts 2:6b). Although the primary loyalty and identity of all Christians, of course, is found in the core Tradition that unites us all in Christ, we still celebrate the fact that blacks sing the Tradition in lively spirituals, while Quakers experience it through silence, and Pentecostals shout, Hallelujah! and pray in tongues. We also can respect and accept our fellow Christians whose tradition calls on them to expect an imminent Second Coming, or burn draft cards, or worship with candles and incense all night on Easter Eve. We only ask of persons in all traditions that they keep themselves and their traditions open to the judging, transforming Source of Tradition, and help him re-form it so that he may continue to be seen clearly in it.

"Traditioning" in the Local Church

If we are to be faithful to the Tradition and effective in doing theology as individuals, we need the help of our local congregation. Individuals do not have traditions—groups do. "Traditioning" is one aspect of doing theology that must be done in a group. So we must join with others in our congregation to engage in the following tasks.

1. *Teach and learn Tradition and the traditions.* To make intelligent use of tradition as a guideline for doing theology, we need to know the Source of our faith in the dynamic, self-renewing Word of God, and the ways in which this Tradition has been interpreted and expressed down through history. The Christian faith has a content, and we and our children must know it if we are to be able to test our private interpretations against Tradition.

The core of Tradition may be taught through ancient and modern creeds, such as the sign of the fish,[2] the Apostles' and the Nicene Creeds, and the World Council of Churches' affirmation, "Jesus Christ, God and Savior." Key Scripture passages (such as John 3:16; Matt. 22:37-39) and the parables of the prodigal son and the good Samaritan are helpful also.

When it comes to the traditions, however, those identified on the tree diagram are only a few of the principal ones. Only time and interest will limit our study of the many forms in which the faith has been wrapped. Our starting point should be our own tradition, whence the religious content of our spectacles comes. We need to know *why* we are Baptist, Methodist, or Presbyterian, and what it means to have our roots there.

Our questions can then be the stimulus to further study. Why do some churches have a central pulpit, and others a divided chancel? Why are some taught that to smoke and drink is wrong, while others do not make an issue of it? Why are some Christians conscientious objectors? Is Christ really present in the bread and wine of Communion? What is a "call"? Why do some churches use prayer books while others pray spontaneously? Why are there Christians on both sides of the abortion issue? Should women be ordained?

Christians respond in different ways, in part because their traditions have handled these questions differently. Knowing the stance of our own tradition, and knowing that of others who differ from us, gives us a more sound basis on which to do our own theology. To enable people to work out their own beliefs, our churches need to provide courses, resources, and opportunity for study and dialogue.

2. *Participate in the traditioning process.* Learning our tradition must not be simply a recitation of historical facts or the memorization of belief statements. All traditional forms and doctrines are only imperfect and culturally conditioned expressions of the living Tradition. They thus require reinterpretation in light of new experience through which God makes himself known to us. Hence, it is also our task to participate with God in translating the Word into contemporary forms that speak in a vital way to people in today's diverse cultural situations. Through creating new patterns of worship, art forms, religious symbols and imagery, stories, and life-styles, we engage in "traditioning."

How can we make the kernel of our faith meaningful to

people in our time? It may be through developing a rite to support divorced persons,[3] or perhaps by creating a series of banners with contemporary symbols and slogans. Some may wish to constitute a communal living arrangement, basing life together on daily worship and a covenant with God and with each other. We might bring an offering of soft drink cans to the altar, to be sent to the President with a request for legislation to ban throwaway containers. Perhaps we will rewrite the service of baptism. We may develop a congregational mission statement, based on images of the church in Scripture and tradition, and formulate action goals and strategies to implement it.

We must use all our creative gifts to enable the Tradition to break out of outdated forms and be expressed in vital new images, words, and actions.

3. *Overcome barriers that separate the traditions.* Because the creative Word of God has been embodied in each of the traditions, we have much to learn from all of them. Some aspects of the Tradition are expressed more clearly in one tradition than in another. But we often are so encased in our own tradition that our vision of the others is obscured, and our resources for doing theology are thus unnecessarily limited. Barriers of doctrine, worship, organization, and custom needlessly divide us and must be overcome, so that we can see through one another's spectacles and learn from one another's experience. We need to realize that faithful response to the Tradition is a more basic responsibility than is rigid adherence to a particular tradition.

We must teach and learn one another's traditions in our churches and thereby become better able to accept that we all belong together within the larger Tradition. We will be aided in doing our own theology if we know why some Lutherans practice closed communion, what Catholics really believe about the Virgin Mary, and how charismatics practice faith healing. Such things can be learned through visits, exchanges, and the use of study books, films, and resource persons from other denominations.

4. *Cultivate theological pluralism.* When the varying traditions are understood as culturally conditioned expressions of, and human responses to, God's self-revelation, doctrinal diversity becomes a gift of God. As the several hues of the rainbow beautify the horizon, so do different faith perspectives enrich our vision of God's truth. It was not until the blind men combined their experience that they discovered the object they were touching was not a rope or a tree, but an elephant. If we insist on one narrow interpretation as the "true view," we severely restrict our understanding of what God has been saying to his people.

We can affirm all the traditions as evidence of the church's faithfulness in the traditioning process and as confirmation of God's revelations in the past. But we ought not to venerate any of them in ways that lead to intolerance or exclusivism. To give one's loyalty solely to the tradition of one denomination or viewpoint, while it may seem to be orthodox and proper, actually could become quite heretical, since it could blind us to the activity of God in other traditions and in the traditioning process of the present. Although one gains a sense of Christian identity through belonging to one of the traditions, a too-strict fidelity to it can make one deaf to the living Tradition.

So in our churches, we need to welcome different points of view. We can encourage those from a Church of God, Congregational, or Catholic background to tell it as they see it. We can serve Communion in various ways, and baptize both by immersion and by sprinkling. We can stimulate diversity of opinion in our classes and discussions. And we can maintain unity and community in the midst of this, *provided* our primary commitment is to the Christ of Tradition, who commanded us to "love one another; even

109

as I have loved you" (John 13:34). Faithfulness to the Tradition enables us to celebrate the pluralism of traditions.

"Traditioning" in the Adams Family

When this kind of traditioning is taking place in our churches, we will have the skills, outlook, and resources for making use of it in situations like the one currently faced by the Adams.

Walter's dissatisfaction with his work, for example, could be eased considerably by an awareness of the Protestant concept of vocation developed by Martin Luther. Protesting against the double standard by which the work of priests and nuns was seen as more holy than that of farmers and merchants, Luther insisted on the sacredness of all life. He contended that God calls his people to serve him in society, as well as in the church. Walter is called to love God and other persons through his job. This, rather than personal reward or advancement, is the primary purpose of work and the source of self-fulfillment. If he can turn his attention from personal snubs and office irritations to ways to benefit his customers and co-workers, he will find his work taking on meaning and purpose again. This insight can come to him through his tradition.

In his role as father, one stream of tradition would reinforce Walter's inflexible, authoritarian stance. Most church traditions grew up in feudal times when the all-powerful God was seen as the model for arbitrary rule. The authority of those in command all down the line, including the father of the family, thus stemmed from God. Walter therefore feels justified in ordering David to stay in his room to do homework or turn himself in to the police. But this autocratic tradition needs to be tested against the Tradition, embodied in the forgiving father of the prodigal son, and against contemporary experience, which seems to support mutuality, empathy, and compromise as the more loving, human way of relating in the family. Walter must do some traditioning to develop a creative new approach to David that will maintain his authority, without being authoritarian, and that will be loving, though not permissive.

With regard to his inner struggle for self-esteem, Walter needs to recognize that it is only recently in competitive American society that self-worth has become closely tied to personal achievement. In the Christian tradition, the worth of the individual is grounded in God's accepting love and in belonging within the community of faith. While rewarding those who "make it," our contemporary culture exacts an enervating toll from people like Walter, who do not. This need not happen, though, if he can rediscover the Tradition, which affirms, "You are my son, today I have begotten you" (Ps. 2:7b).

There is a whole host of women in the Christian tradition with whom Marge can identify.[4] In her concern for her son, she might gain inspiration from Monica, the mother of St. Augustine. In her efforts to be supportive of her troubled husband, she could find encouragement in the model of Katherine Von Bora, who left the convent to marry Martin Luther. In her determination to be her own person, her example might be Anne Hutchinson, who suffered imprisonment and banishment from the Massachusetts Bay Colony in her fight for religious liberty. In her desire to serve through the church, she might seek the guidance of Clare, a co-worker with St. Francis of Assisi and the founder of the order of Poor Clares.

As Marge struggles to affirm her worth as a person, apart from her role as mother and housewife, and to develop her talents, she can take heart from the strain in the Christian tradition that values the "varieties of gifts"

111

(I Cor. 12:4) and their contribution to "the common good" (12:7) in the body of Christ. It will encourage her to learn that wherever the Christian gospel has spread in the world, the status of women has been improved and their abilities and worth have been recognized. Even though the history of the church is full of instances of discrimination against women, she will see these human, cultural wrappings torn away by the Tradition, which affirms that "there is neither male nor female; for you are all one in Christ Jesus" (Gal. 3:28).

The element in the Christian tradition that may strike closest to David's condition is commitment. It is because his life lacks a clear purpose that he has damaged his relationships, endangered his future, and become despondent. It will help him to look at persons who, taking their cue from Jesus, who "set his face to go to Jerusalem" (Luke 9:51), have stood firmly for their convictions. For example, St. Francis resisted the demands of his wealthy father and left home to serve the poor and outcast. John Wycliffe withstood heavy persecution when he translated the Bible into English. Roger Williams left Massachusetts to found the colony of Rhode Island, to insure religious liberty for himself and others. Martin Luther King, Jr., persevered to the death in his leadership in the civil rights struggle of black Americans.

Perhaps David is ready to recognize that he lacks this commitment and to surrender his life to Christ, who can supply it. If so, he is being confronted by the Source of Tradition who says, "If any [one] would come after me, let him deny himself and take up his cross and follow me" (Mark 8:34b-35). A response to this invitation has been the beginning of a new life for persons from St. Augustine to John Bunyan, and from Teresa of Avila to General William Booth. The Tradition insists that self-actualization, or salvation, is not something that can be earned, achieved, or developed. It is a gift of God's grace and is received when one decides to give his or her life to Christ and his purposes.

The example of his fathers and mothers in the faith, the message in the "Jesus, the Good Shepherd" stained-glass window, and the call to confession in the worship service, all summon David to take this step. Each time a person accepts Christ as Lord and Savior, he or she is continuing the traditioning process by giving the Tradition a new wrapping. For the traditioning process enables the Word to become flesh (John 1:14) in forms of architecture, worship, symbol, doctrine, and human life. The choice David now faces is whether to invite the Word to become flesh in him.

"Traditioning" is translating the heart of the Tradition into language and forms that enliven our experience with Christian meaning. God's Spirit inspires traditioning, but we must do the work. Meanings like these will help the Adams family gain perspective on themselves and their situation and discover new approaches to their needs and problems. The same can be true for all of us.

Tradition may seem dead, but God wants to work with us in giving it new life.

TO DO IN PRIVATE

Reflect on a film, book, event, or scripture you have encountered, as soon as possible after the experience. Sit down with your journal and follow these steps:

1. *What happened . . .*
    a. In the experience? Relive it and write down a brief synopsis.
    b. In you? Recall your inner feelings and responses and write them down. Use "feeling" words to describe them.

2. *With whom did you identify?*
   a. Which character did you follow with most interest? Whom were you rooting for, feeling sorry for, or seeing yourself in?
   b. What was there about that person that caused you to like, support, or sympathize with him or her?
   c. What is there about you that draws you to that person? How are you similar?
3. *What beliefs are involved?*
   a. What is the key insight conveyed by the experience? What statement about the meaning of life is communicated?
   b. In what ways does this central message support or deny your basic beliefs?
   c. What do you believe about the issue(s) it raises?
4. *How is traditioning needed, or how is it taking place?*
   a. How does the message of this experience measure up, in the light of Tradition?
   b. Was traditioning involved in the event? If so, in what ways? If not, how could the issue or message be expressed so that you and others would want to make a faith response?
5. *What is your response?*
   a. How did you feel about the way the event turned out?
   b. How would you have changed it to make persons or actions more faithful to Tradition?
   c. If you were to be faithful to the Tradition encountered in this experience, what must you do, change, or try to become?

Close your time of meditation with prayer, asking God to help you become more appreciative of the traditions, more sensitive to the Tradition, and more capable and creative in doing your own traditioning. To help clarify your thoughts and feelings, write your prayers in your journal.

TO DO IN A GROUP

Everyone should have a copy of the Lord's Supper liturgy and a communion bulletin. The order of worship for another service, such as baptism or marriage, may be substituted if you wish. Write these instructions on the board, and then write responses to the questions in your journals.

1. Select one prayer, reading, or statement of faith from the liturgy. (Do this publicly so that all the major elements in the service are examined.)

2. What is it saying? Paraphrase it in words that will carry meaning for you and the people you know. Then state its central message in one succinct sentence.

3. What does it imply about (a) the kind of persons we are? (b) God's attitude toward us? (c) who we are called to be?

4. What dialogue between you and God does this stimulate? Use this format to write:

> God: (your name), *you*———
> You: *God, I*———

5. What situation in your life is addressed by this prayer and its message?

6. How would your life be different if you really took this message to heart?

When members have finished writing, begin to share. Use the following questions to guide the discussion.

1. Did you find this traditional liturgy meaningful? Why, or why not?

2. Give your one-sentence summaries of each prayer or reading. How well does each capture the meaning and address your situation and need?

3. Give your responses to question 3 above. List these on the board and summarize them in a brief statement of what this liturgy says about God, human nature, and human potential.

115

4. Do you agree with this statement? If not, how would you change it? Evaluate your revised statement in light of the four guidelines for doing theology—Scripture, tradition, reason, and experience.

5. Share your "dialogues with God." Respond to each with support, understanding, suggestion, or confrontation, as needed.

6. Share your responses to the questions on life situations addressed, and changes called for.

7. Have you found this exercise in traditioning meaningful? In what ways?

8. How can your group lead the congregation in making this and other forms of your life together (worship, organization, fellowship, service) more meaningful by translating traditional patterns into lively new expressions?

Close with a litany. After each person in turn says "I believe—" following with an affirmation he or she believes in, the group responds with, "We affirm you in your belief."

OTHER EXERCISES

1. "Traditioning the Creed." Read over the Apostles Creed (or another) and select a phrase that gives expression to a historic Christian dogma—for instance, "from thence he shall come to judge the quick and the dead." Look up the key words in a concordance, Bible dictionary, or word book to discover their scriptural basis and traditional meaning. Then write out the phrase in your own words.

Now ask yourself: How does Christ come to me? How do I hope he will come in the future? How do I experience judgment in my life? How is Christ's coming a judgment on me? How does he offer me hope and deliverance at the same time? What persons and situations around me need this word of both judgment and hope? How can I communicate it in a way they can understand? Write your responses, and share with the group. Do similar reflections on other traditional doctrines.

2. "Translating a Vision."[5] A vision that has been part of the Judeo-Christian tradition for centuries is that of "shalom." It speaks of right relationships, peace, justice, and well-being for all people. Its source is God; its embodiment is the covenant relationship and the caring community; its mandate is to work with God to meet human needs, enable personal wholeness, and establish global harmony and justice.

Write a fantasy in which one segment of your world (family, work community, nation) gives full expression to the shalom vision.

Then ask: What factors in this situation are blocking the realization of this fantasy? What factors are enabling it? What concrete steps could I take to strengthen the enabling forces and weaken the blocking forces? Who can I get to join me? What commitments will I now make to translate the shalom vision into action in my situation? How do I plan to do theology with deeds as well as words?

117

Epilogue

The Adams Family Achieves Shared Meaning

Finding they lacked the resources and skills to solve their problems themselves, the Adams wisely turned for help to their church, the intended setting for doing theology. Mr. and Mrs. Adams took their dilemma to their sharing group, David had a long talk with the youth fellowship counselor, and together, they had several conferences with their pastor. We will not examine the process in detail, but here is what happened as a result.

The elder Adams discovered they were not alone. Other parents in their group told of teen-agers who were lacking direction and testing parental authority. Other men expressed feelings of frustration and disillusionment about their work. Marge's friends openly declared their resentment at being boxed in and denied their own "selfhood." Some shared ways they had tried to deal with these concerns—family therapy, divorce, a job change, hobbies, volunteer service. Walter and Marge came away with new hope and with some concrete ideas about next steps.

David found his youth counselor to be an understanding friend and soon began to open up. In response to tactful questions, he was able to express his thoughts about the reactions of Cindy and his parents. He also received insight into what forgiveness, reconciliation, freedom and responsibility, and discipleship are all about. He never had given much thought to a connection between the Christian faith and his personal struggles, but after hearing the youth leader's comments, he knew he wanted to investigate it further.

The fact that their pastor came to their home was very helpful. The presence of a third party who cared, encouraged them to try harder to say what they really meant, to moderate their emotions, and to listen to one another. As the pastor reflected back what they were saying, they heard one another more clearly, felt the others' hurts, and realized how they all were imposing their own needs and expectations on the others.

Through a problem-solving technique, the pastor guided them in identifying needs, key issues, factors favorable to or interfering with a solution, and steps that would enable them to reach their goals as a family. Each was helped to decide on ways to accomplish personal aims, while at the same time supporting the others and enhancing family solidarity. By her example of responsive listening, identification of feelings, and clarification of intended meanings, the pastor encouraged the Adams to learn to use these communication skills themselves. And through reference to biblical images, themes, and persons, she helped them discover crossing' points and similarities between these and their own experience.

These initial encounters led the Adams back into active participation in the adult Bible class, youth fellowship, and worship services. They became involved as a family in a church service project, collecting canned goods for a common pantry and helping plan a "hunger banquet." This experience led David to volunteer for a weekend work camp, and Marge began to experiment with vegetarian recipes, which in turn inspired her husband to plant a garden the next spring.

Walter also became interested in helping a day-care center in the inner city, going in once a week to repair equipment and do bookkeeping. He began to look forward to the evenings and weekends because of his involvement with his garden, the volunteer service, and the Bible class. When the vegetables were ready, he took on the task of canning and freezing in order to free Marge to continue her ceramics class and to get ready for the fall semester. He had more enthusiasm for his job, too. The idea that work is our service to God and our opportunity for witness helped him become less concerned with pleasing his boss, more interested in really knowing the people he dealt with, and more resolute in standing by his convictions. He had accepted the reality that he wouldn't rise any higher in his job, but he concluded that his gifts were well-used and decided to stay on until retirement. He began to ask God each day to help him in "rendering service with a good will as to the Lord" (Eph. 6:7).

Yes, Marge was going back to college to get a business degree. The support from her family and sharing group had given her the incentive she needed. But increasingly, she was convinced that she could serve God best and find the greatest personal fulfillment by opening her own shop. The ceramics class was the first step, and the degree would be the second. With some promise that her own aspirations would be met, Marge was better able to respond to the feelings and needs of her family. She found inspiration for her new lease on life in the fortitude of Queen Esther, the image of the mustard seed, the example of her pastor, who had sought training for ministry after raising her family, and the support of the other women in her sharing group.

David, however, was becoming aware that more schooling was not for him, at least for the present. He would graduate from high school, but then he wanted to do some traveling before deciding on any future direction. Though his parents were not happy about this decision, they saw how restless he was and, reflecting on their own "locked in"[1] feelings due to actions taken too early, they gave him their blessing.

Through attending the human sexuality weekend at church, David had gained a new perspective on his own sexuality and his goals for relationships with girls. He shared these insights with Cindy, and though she was wary and would not accept a date, they parted as friends. With this encouragement that their relationship might soon be fully restored, he became more cheerful at home and renewed contacts with his other friends.

While associating with the youth in the church group, David had begun to find that there was more to life than he thus far had realized. These kids had fun, but he could tell that some of them, at least, were trying consciously to live for Christ, and this appealed to him. When he was with them he was stimulated to try to visualize his life fitting into a larger purpose. The words of Jesus, "Follow me, and I will make you fishers of men" (Matt. 4:19), sounded as though they were meant for him, and he was pondering what a yes to this call might mean.

Intentional involvement in their community of faith had turned things around for the Adams family. Through the worship and study programs, their faith was enriched, and they learned how to translate it into everyday experience. In small groups they met people who cared and who offered them support, guidance, and a challenge to grow. In church activities they found opportunity to develop and express their gifts and to engage in God's misson of love and liberation in the world.

But this is only part of the story. For in that same church the Adams encountered some people who felt uncomfortable when sharing their problems, and others who saw no connection between Sunday worship and the teachings of the Bible and the church, and their daily lives. There were also conflicts galore—over everything from the sponsorship of a halfway house for paroled convicts and the issues of premarital sex and capital punishment, to the choice of choral anthems.

Although the Adams did not find much agreement in their church they did find people who respected and cared about one another. Diversity did not bother them because their unity rested on their common experience with God in Christ and on the mutual love and trust this generated. They did not need to insist on conformity, because they found deep acceptance in community. They respected and even enjoyed their differences because they were secure in themselves and in the covenant that bound them to one another and to Christ. This enabled them all to be free to discover their own meanings, do their own traditioning, and act on their own convictions. They had learned to feel comfortable with conflict and to try to see through the others' "spectacles."

In this setting the Adams were encouraged to do their own theology in the company of other Christians. They were introduced to new biblical images and themes and confronted with aspects of Tradition and the traditions that enriched their own limited perspectives. They found themselves questioning and being questioned, risking and supporting the risks of others, growing and stimulating growth. They had discovered shared meaning and a sense of koinonia,[2] both in their church and in their own household.

The experience of the Adams family can be ours when we engage seriously and regularly with other Christians in the task of working out our own beliefs.

Notes

Chapter 3 Experience—The Raw Material for Doing Theology

1. Data for diagram based on Hierarchy of Needs in "A Theory of Human Motivation" in *Motivation and Personality*, 2d ed., pp. 35-47, by Abraham H. Maslow. Copyright © 1970 by Abraham H. Maslow. By permission of Harper & Row, Publishers, Inc.

Chapter 4 Reason—The Process of Meaning-Making

1. Neil Postman and Charles Weingartner, *Teaching as a Subversive Activity* (New York: Delacorte Press, 1969), pp. 82-97, contains an account of the experimental basis for this assertion in the work of Adelbert Ames, Jr., Earl Kelley, I. A. Richards, and Robert Rosenthal.
2. The idea for this three-part breakdown has come from C. Ellis Nelson, *Where Faith Begins* (Richmond: John Knox Press, 1967), especially pp. 58-65. © M. E. Bratcher 1967. Used by permission of John Knox Press.
3. Ronald Goldman, *Religious Thinking from Childhood to Adolescence* (New York: The Seabury Press, 1968), p. 1.
4. See Resource List for recommended titles.
5. The concept of "shared meaning" has been developed by psychologists Sherod Miller, Elam W. Nunnally, and Daniel B. Wackman, and is described in *Alive and Aware* (Minneapolis: Interpersonal Communication Programs, 1975). See pp. 110-29 for a description of a training process for developing skill in achieving shared meaning in relationships.

6. The idea for this exercise has come from the "Steppingstones" journal reflection described by Dr. Ira Progoff in *At a Journal Workshop* (New York: Dialogue House Library, 1975), pp. 98-130.
7. This exercise is patterned after the one described in the chapter "Dialogue with Works," Progoff, pp. 178-93.
8. The idea for these exercises comes from a discussion of "Paradise: Lost and Found," in Sam Keen and Anne Valley Fox, *Telling Your Story: A Guide to Who You Are and Who You Can Be.* Copyright © 1973 by Sam Kean and Anne Bartlett. (New York: Doubleday and Co., Inc., 1973), pp. 145-48. Reprinted by permission of Doubleday & Co. and The Sterling Lord Agency, Inc.

Chapter 5 Scripture—An Object of Faith or a Resource for Faith?

1. Douglas E. Wingeier, "Christian Education as Faith Translation," *The Living Light* 14, no. 3 (Fall 1977), pp. 397-98. For a fuller description of these and other ways of approaching the Bible, see Dorothy Jean Furnish, *Exploring the Bible with Children* (Nashville: Abingdon Press, 1975), pp. 28-39.
2. This diagram first appeared in a slightly different form in Wingeier, "Christian Education," p. 398.
3. See Resource List for suggested titles.
4. See Edward P. Blair, *Abingdon Bible Handbook* (Nashville: Abingdon Press, 1975), pp. 56-61, for a fuller treatment of the guidelines discussed in this section.
5. See Resource List for suggestions.
6. This exercise and the idea behind it are adapted from Karl A. Olsson, *Find Your Self in the Bible* (Minneapolis: Augsburg Publishing House, 1974). Copyright 1974. Used by permission of Augsburg Publishing House.
7. Adapted from Ross Snyder, *Risk, The Ministry of Meaning,* vol. I, nos. 3 and 4 (1965), pp. 175-79, used by permission of World Council of Churches.

Chapter 6 Tradition—Dead or Alive?

1. Wingeier, "Christian Education." Portions of this chapter are a revised and expanded version of pp. 399-402 of that article.
2. The Greek word for fish is *ichthus,* the letters of which are the first letters of the words, Jesus Christ, Son of God, Savior. This was their creed.
3. See *Ritual in a New Day: An Invitation* (Nashville: Abingdon, 1976) for examples of this and other rituals to provide symbolic meaning for contemporary experience.
4. Edith Deen, *Great Women of the Christian Faith* (New York: Harper & Brothers, 1959) contains brief accounts of the lives of these and other women significant in Christian history.

5. Additional resources for this reflection and others on the same theme may be found in the participant's and leader's manuals of *Teaching Toward a Faithful Vision*, produced by the Task Force on Christian Education for World Peace (Nashville: Discipleship Resources, 1977).

Epilogue

1. This phrase is used by Gail Sheehy in *Passages* (New York: E. P. Dutton, 1976) to describe a life pattern in which young people decide early on marriage and career, largely to meet parental expectations, only to begin to feel bored and stifled at mid-life. See pp. 182-89, 217-23.
2. A Greek word meaning fellowship, used to describe the church as a caring community.

Resource List

A. About Doing Theology

Christian, C. W. *Shaping Your Faith: A Guide to a Personal Theology.* Waco, Tex.: Word Books, 1973.

Evans, Robert A., and Parker, Thomas D. *Christian Theology: A Case Study Approach.* New York: Harper & Row, 1976.

Harkness, Georgia. *Understanding the Christian Faith.* Nashville: Abingdon-Cokesbury Press, 1947.

Holmes, Urban T., III. *To Speak of God: Theology for Beginners.* New York: The Seabury Press, 1974.

Hordern, William E. *A Layman's Guide to Protestant Theology.* New York: The Macmillan Co., 1972.

Jennings, Theodore W., Jr. *Introduction to Theology.* Philadelphia: Fortress Press, 1976.

Koyama, Kosuke. *Waterbuffalo Theology.* Maryknoll, N.Y.: Orbis Books, 1974.

Menninger, Karl. *Whatever Became of Sin?* New York: Hawthorn Books, 1973.

Tillich, Paul. *Dynamics of Faith.* New York: Harper & Brothers, 1958.

B. About Interpreting Scripture

Anderson, Bernhard W. *Understanding the Old Testament.* 3d ed. Englewood Cliffs, N.J.: Prentice-Hall, 1975.

Boelter, Francis W. *The Covenant People of God.* Nashville: Tidings, 1971.

Brown, Robert McAfee. *The Bible Speaks to You.* Philadelphia: The Westminster Press, 1955.

DeWolf, L. Harold. *The Enduring Message of the Bible.* New York: Harper & Brothers, 1960.

Everding, H. Edward, Jr., and Wilbanks, Dana W. *Decision-Making and the Bible.* Valley Forge, Pa.: Judson Press, 1975.

Kee, Howard Clark; Young, Franklin W.; and Froelich, Karlfried. *Understanding the New Testament.* 3d ed. Englewood Cliffs, N.J.: Prentice-Hall, 1973.

Smart, James D. *The Strange Silence of the Bible in the Church.* Philadelphia: The Westminster Press, 1970.

Wink, Walter. *The Bible in Human Transformation.* Philadelphia: Fortress Press, 1973.

C. Helps for Interpreting Scripture

Black, Matthew, and Rowley, H. H. eds. *Peake's Commentary on the Bible.* Rev. ed. Don Mills, Ontario: Thomas Nelson, 1976.

Blair, Edward P. *Abingdon Bible Handbook.* Nashville: Abingdon Press, 1975.

Buttrick, George A., commentary ed. *The Interpreter's Bible,* vols. I-XII. Nashville: Abingdon Press, 1956

Buttrick, George A., dictionary ed. *The Interpreter's Dictionary of the Bible,* vols. I-IV. Nashville: Abingdon Press, 1962. Crim, Keith, gen. ed. Supplementary Vol. Nashville: Abingdon, 1976.

Hendricks, J. Sherrell; Sease, Gene E.; Titus, Eric L.; and Wiggins, James B. *Christian Word Book.* Nashville: Graded Press, 1968.

Joy, Charles R. *Harper's Topical Concordance.* Rev. enl. ed. New York: Harper & Row, 1962.

Miller, Madeleine S., and Miller, J. Lane. *Harper's Bible Dictionary.* 4th ed. New York: Harper & Brothers, 1956.

RSV Handy Concordance, The. Grand Rapids: Zondervan Publishing House, 1962.

von Allmen, Jean Jacques. *A Companion to the Bible.* New York: Oxford University Press, 1958.

D. Sources of Exercises for Doing Theology in Groups

Coleman, Lyman. *Serendipity* Series. Waco, Tex.: Word, Inc., 1971.

Hall, Brian P. *Value Clarification as Learning Process: A Guidebook.* Paramus, N.J.: Paulist/Newman Press, 1973.

Howe, Leland W. *Taking Charge of Your Life.* Niles, Ill.: Argus Communications, 1977.

Keen, Sam, and Fox, Anne Valley. *Telling Your Story: A Guide to Who You Are and Who You Can Be.* New York: Doubleday & Co., 1973.

Minor, Harold D., ed. *Techniques and Resources for Guiding Adult Groups.* Nashville-New York: Abingdon Press, 1972.

Mitchell, Kenneth J. *To Know, To Trust, To Grow.* Nashville: Graded Press, 1976.

Seifert, Harvey, and Seifert, Lois. *Liberation of Life: Growth Exercises in Meditation and Action.* Nashville: The Upper Room, 1976.

Simon, Sidney B. *Meeting Yourself Halfway.* Niles, Ill.: Argus Communications, 1974.

Snyder, Ross. *Risk, The Ministry of Meaning,* vol. I, nos. 3 and 4, 1965.

Task Force on Christian Education for World Peace. *Teaching Toward a Faithful Vision.* Participant's Manual and Leader's Manual. Nashville: Discipleship Resources, 1977.